Connect
To The Light

Focus Wheel Workbook

"Finally, brothers and sisters, whatever is true, whatever is noble, whatever is right, whatever is pure, whatever is lovely, whatever is admirable—if anything is excellent or praiseworthy—think about such things."
—Philippians 4:8 (NIV)

This Focus Wheel Workbook belongs to and is prayed over

By: _____   Date: _____

Rediscover Truth

Connect To The Light
Focus Wheel Workbook
Receive Joy

Receive Joy Publishing
Naples, Florida, U.S.A.

© 2020 Receive Joy
Carisa Jones, Sylvia Lehmann
All rights reserved.
Cover photography by Steven C. Jones, ©2017

ISBN: 978-0-9988484-9-5

Receive Joy, LLC
www.receivejoy.com
ask@receivejoy.com

YOUR GUIDE FOR USING THE FOCUS WHEEL WORKBOOK

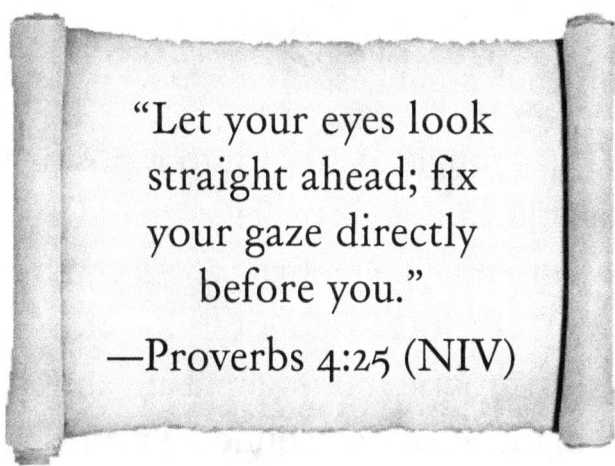

"Let your eyes look straight ahead; fix your gaze directly before you."
—Proverbs 4:25 (NIV)

The *Focus Wheel Workbook* presents you with an easy exercise to engage your belief system, stay in a positive mindset, and pray into the solution.

Encourage yourself to increase your belief in all areas of life by expressing clarity and solid evidence in writing. As you increase your belief, the desired outcome is attainable. You are creating certainty to increase your belief and actively imprint your subconscious. Keep your eyes on the victory, build a solution-oriented mindset, and ultimately receive your desired goals. All the answers and solutions are in you already.

1. Choose a thought or belief you wish to increase. It may be a feeling that is outdated and you wish to update. The first step is to recognize and identify your current belief system. What thoughts do you repeatedly think? What sayings did you hear over and over growing

up? For example, "God takes better care of others than of me," or money is yet to come to you in abundance or you have reluctance when giving. While growing up, you may have heard repeatedly "We can't afford it." You may feel a tightness in your chest thinking of your self-worth or finances.

2. Rephrase the old thought pattern into a positive affirmation that you wish to anchor into your belief system. Replace your thought with a solution-oriented belief that serves you better. For example, "I am worthy of God's love." Better serving affirmations to increase your belief system around money are: I am abundant. Money flows light and easy to me. I have an abundant mindset

3. Fill in the circle with the new, more powerful belief.

4. Fill in the spokes around the statement. List all the reasons why you can have your goal. Aim for 12 or more inspirational statements that help you believe in your new powerful thought. Add solution-oriented actions. All the written declarations help you to focus on the truth of the new belief and show you why you are able to attain your goal. For example:

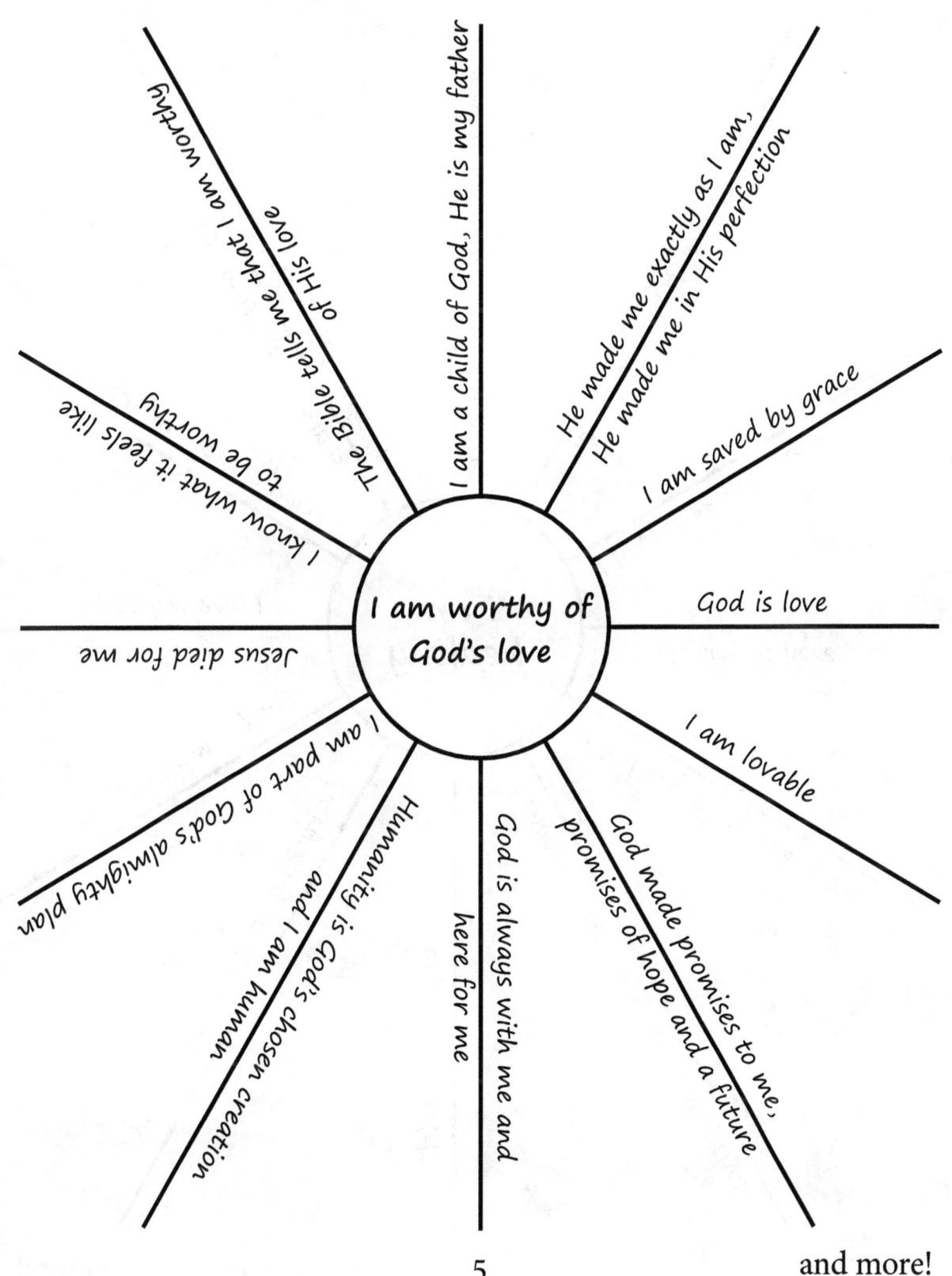

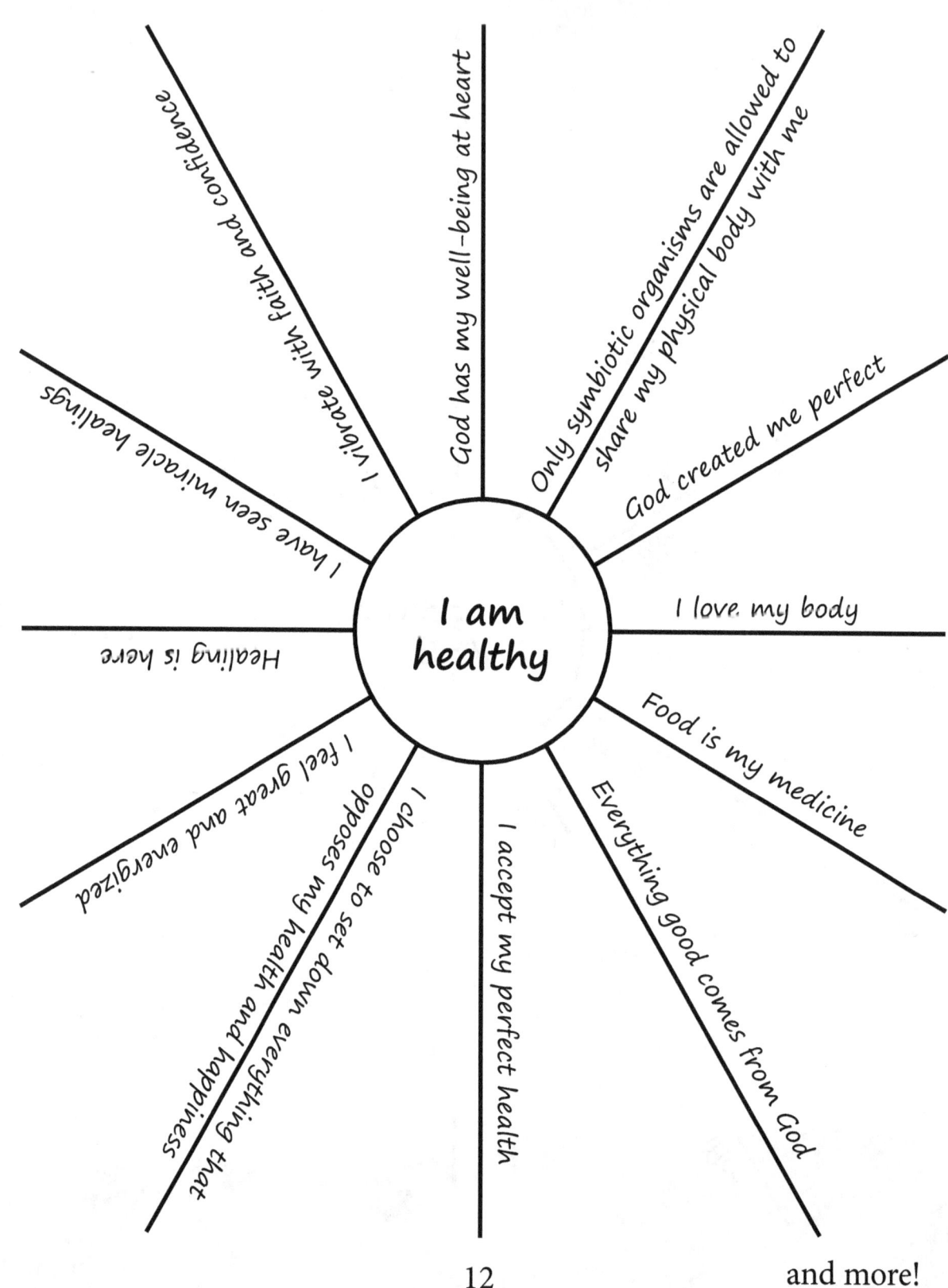

5. Read your new affirmations out loud daily to positively imprint your subconscious.

> "Finally, brothers and sisters, whatever is true, whatever is noble, whatever is right, whatever is pure, whatever is lovely, whatever is admirable—if anything is excellent or praiseworthy—think about such things."
> —Philippians 4:8 (NIV)

Receive Joy collected over 50 beliefs to help you think about excellent and praiseworthy things. Use these empowering statements to increase your belief in all areas of your life.

1. Choose a belief you wish to focus on. Use our suggestions or the blank Focus Wheels following.

2. Fill in the spokes with 12 or more declarations that you can already believe about this empowering thought.

3. If you are yet to come up with enough compelling reasons, flip the page and use some of our suggestions to inspire you.

COMMON BELIEFS THAT SHALL BE ENHANCED AND ANCHORED IN YOUR BELIEF SYSTEM:

1. I am enough
2. I love myself
3. I love my family
4. I am love, I love myself and others
5. I am worthy of God's love
6. I deserve to be happy
7. I see myself as God sees me
8. I see only the good in myself and others
9. I feel excellent
10. I am perfect exactly as I am right now
11. I am beautiful
12. I am healthy
13. I love to exercise
14. I focus on my breath
15. My brain works at its highest function and I have perfect memory

16. I pray
17. I journal daily
18. I meditate
19. I know my gifts and talents
20. I believe in myself
21. I am confident
22. I am a winner
23. I am self-assured
24. I was born to dominate
25. I am successful
26. I am abundant
27. I am financially free
28. I always prosper in everything I do
29. I have faith
30. I have time
31. I know my next step

32. I only listen to God and my all-knowing

33. God always provides

34. I am a cheerful giver

35. I have lovely happy friends who are cheerful givers

36. I have formed valuable partnerships

37. I am worthy to ask for my desires

38. I ask in detail

39. My thoughts attract

40. My words create

41. I receive

42. Everything I ask for I receive

43. I believe in miracles

44. I am responsible for all my decisions

45. I own my life

46. Life is good

47. I am excited about my life

48. I welcome change

49. I live in the now

50. I welcome complete peace

51. All is well all the time

52. I choose to trade in my free will for God's Divine Will

53. God dwells within me

54. I connect to the light of God

55. I am the light

56. I am Word

57. I am free

58. God is in control

59. Jesus did a complete work on the cross

You can always use the following general statements of loving truth and affirmations to add to your Focus Wheel and positive thoughts:

- ♥ I am a child of God
- ♥ God loves me
- ♥ Jesus died for me, He did a complete work on the cross

- ♥ God gave me gifts and talents for my life on earth
- ♥ I focus on the victory in every area of my life
- ♥ If others can do it, so can I
- ♥ I am part of God's divine plan and I have a divine mission to fulfill that only I can do
- ♥ God's timing is now
- ♥ I am a co-creator with God
- ♥ I believe it is possible to create with God
- ♥ It is my birthright
- ♥ I trust myself
- ♥ I am free
- ♥ I know what love feels like
- ♥ I can read and write
- ♥ I have an education
- ♥ It always gets better
- ♥ The best is yet to come
- ♥ I am a good person
- ♥ I lead with kindness
- ♥ I use my resources

- ♥ I practice self-control
- ♥ All is well all the time
- ♥ All things are possible all the time
- ♥ With God all things are possible

> "with God all things are possible."
> —Matthew 19:26b (NIV)

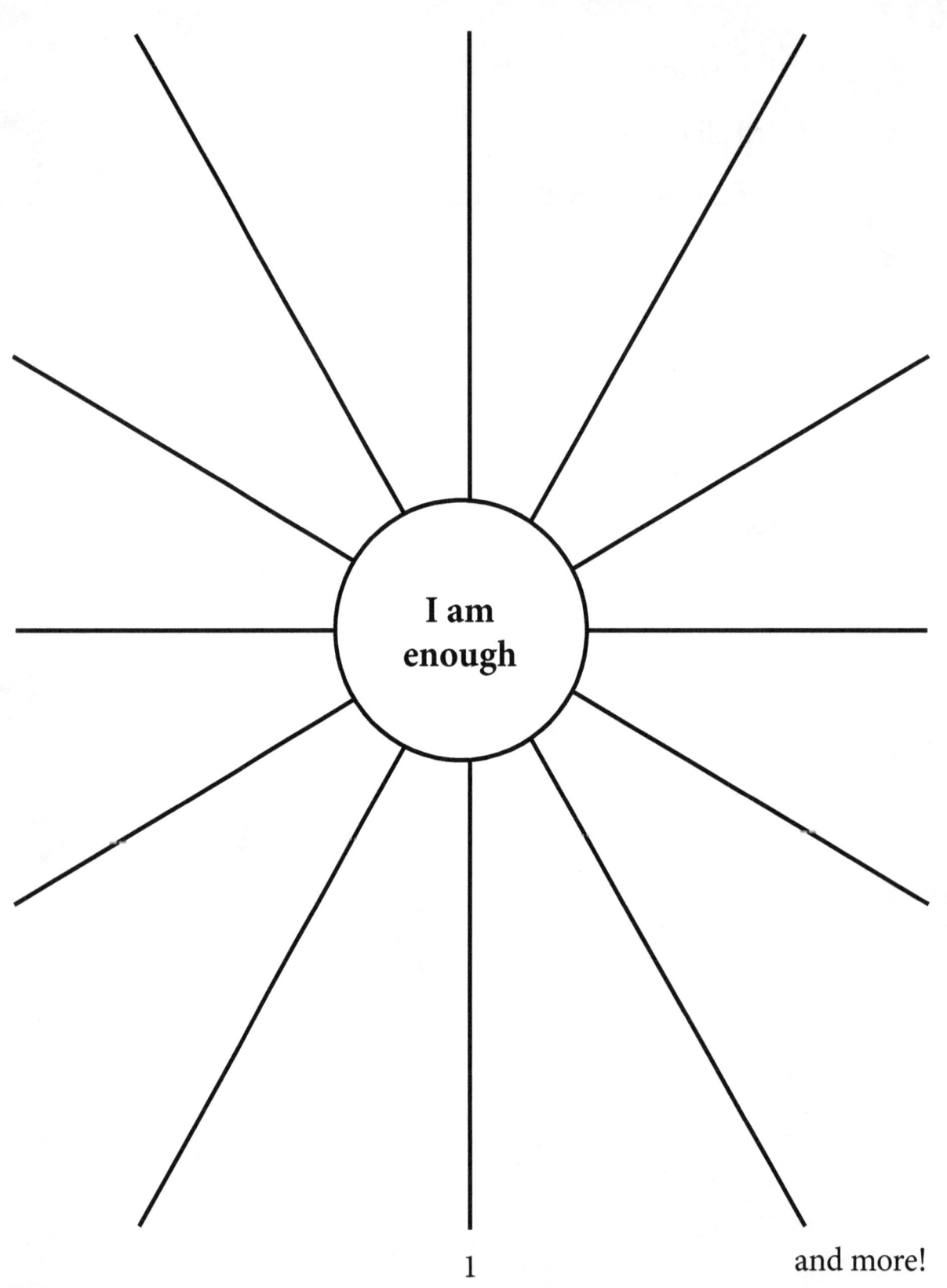

and more!

I am enough

Variations: I am good enough

♥ I am a child of God

♥ God loves me

♥ God gave me gifts and talents for my mission on earth

♥ I am perfect just as I am

♥ I am content

♥ God sustains me

♥ I always make the most of everything

♥ I am always growing and progressing

♥ I am enough and I always will be enough

♥ God gives me everything I require to succeed

♥ My family and friends love me as I am

♥ I know what it feels like to be enough

_____

_____

_____

_____

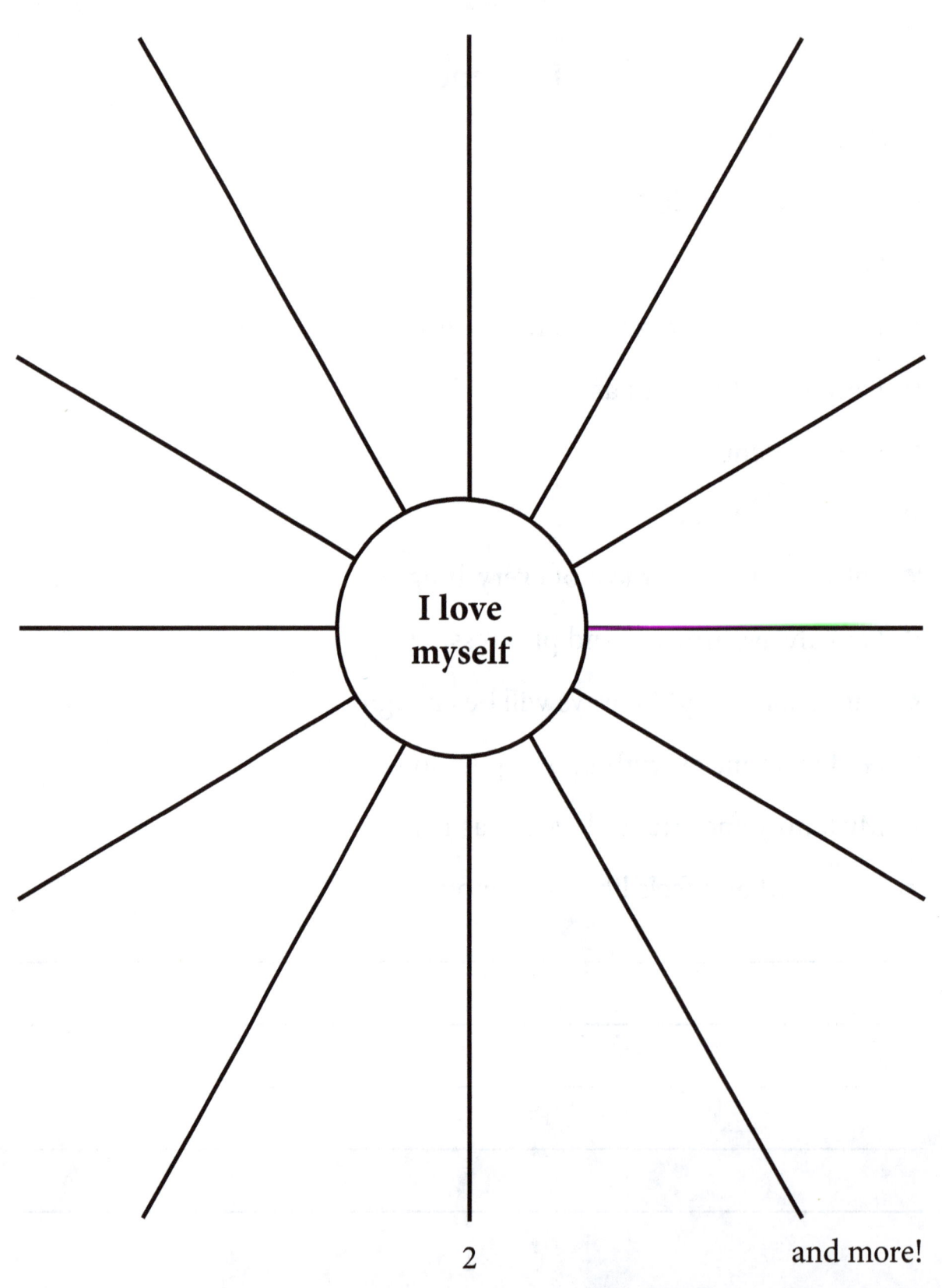

and more!

I love myself

- ♥ God loves me
- ♥ I see myself through God's eyes
- ♥ I am happy to be me
- ♥ I am good to myself
- ♥ I schedule time for myself
- ♥ I have positive thoughts about myself
- ♥ I speak kind words to myself
- ♥ I am my biggest encourager
- ♥ I am perfect just as I am
- ♥ I am my best friend
- ♥ I am happy and content with myself
- ♥ Love flows through me

_____

_____

_____

_____

_____

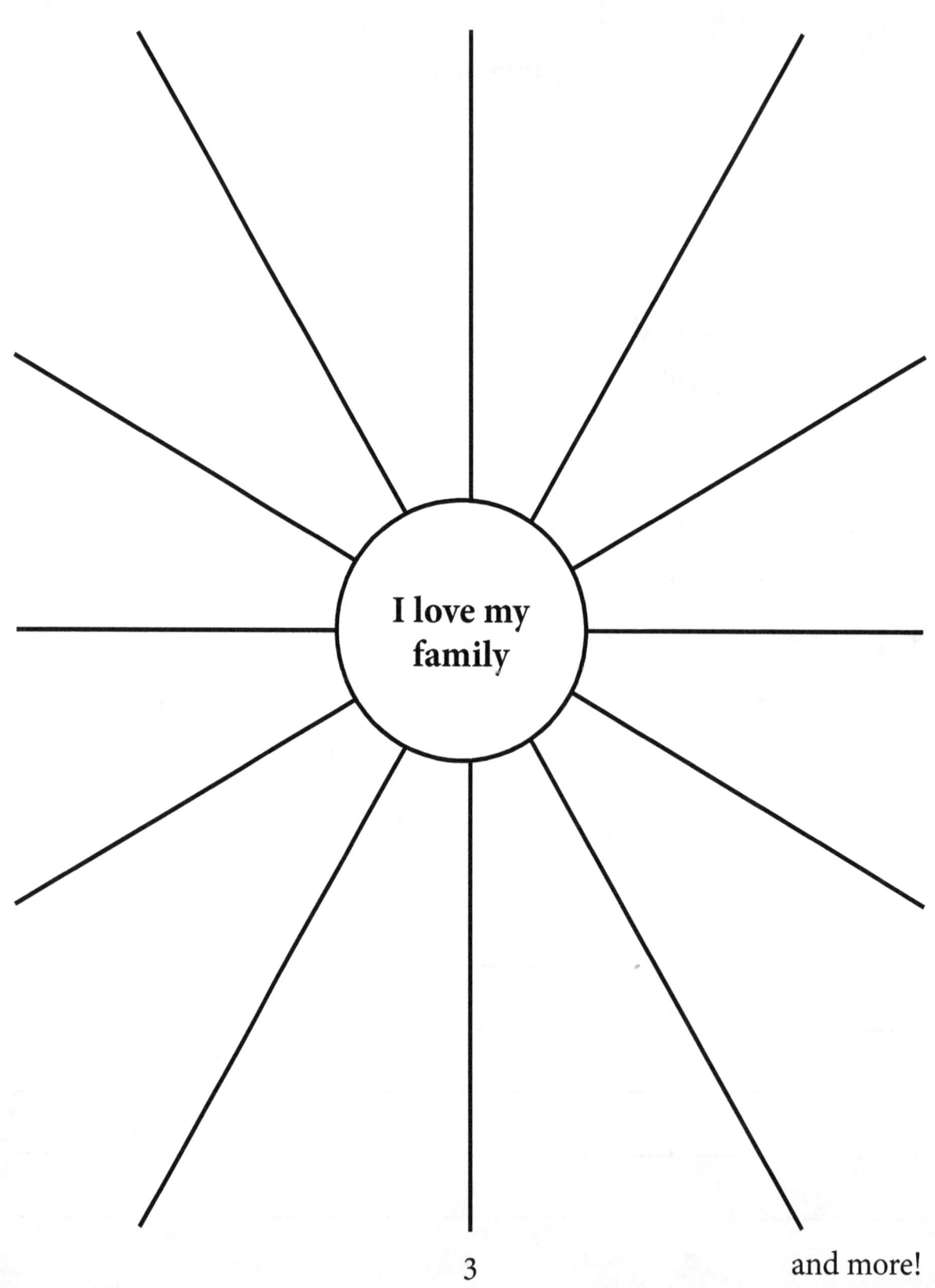

I love my family

and more!

I love my family

- ♥ I can learn something from everyone in my family such as love, kindness, patience, self-control, joy, and compassion
- ♥ My family equipped me with everything I require to form my unique gifts and talents
- ♥ God is part of my family
- ♥ My family members are my friends
- ♥ I enjoy being with my family
- ♥ I celebrate holidays with my family
- ♥ My family and I love each other and grow together
- ♥ Having family feels good
- ♥ It is fun to share love with people close to me
- ♥ There is something special about love shared in a family
- ♥ I am loved by my family
- ♥ Having family is a blessing

_____

_____

_____

_____

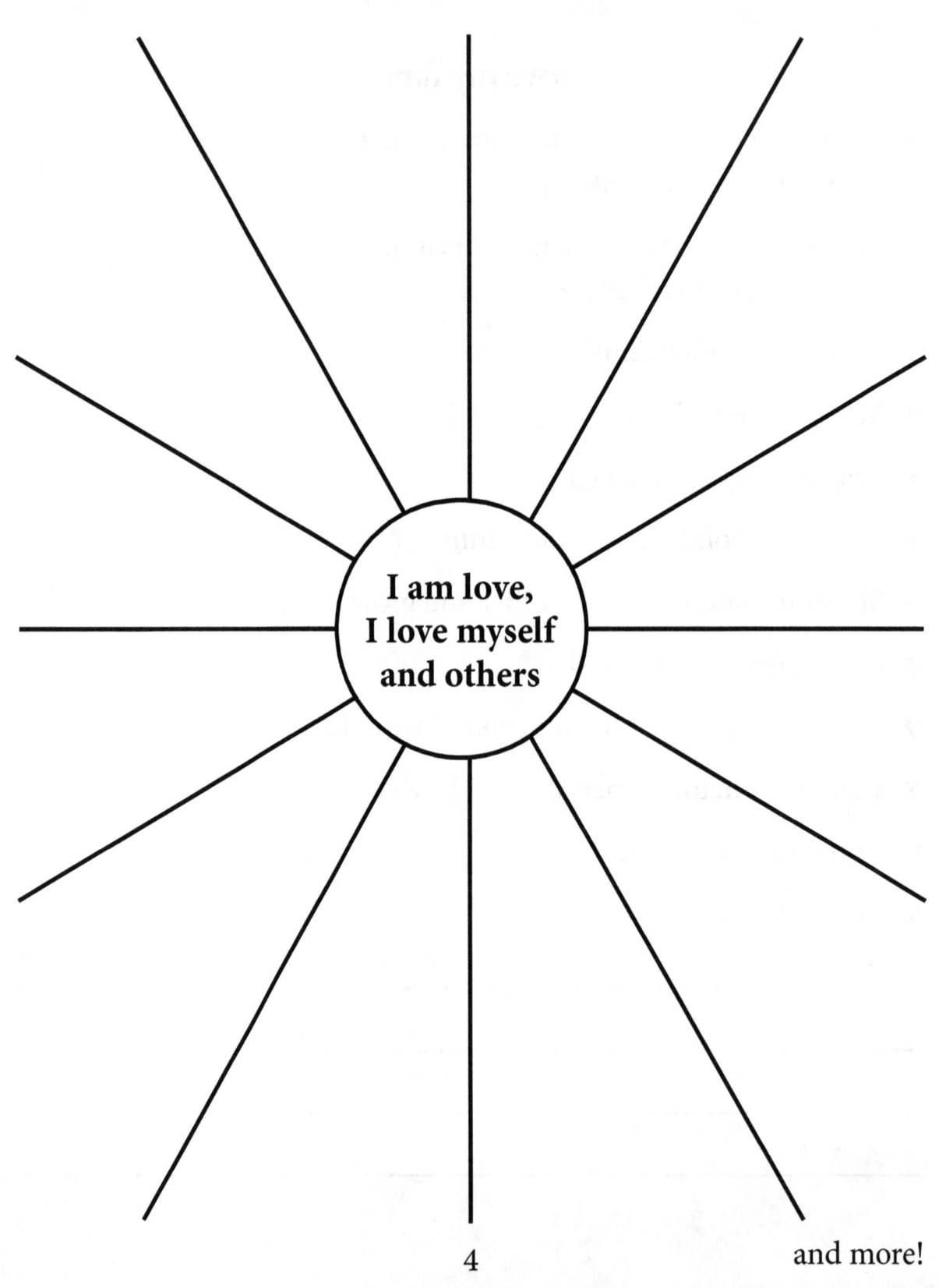

and more!

I am love, I love myself and others

- ♥ Love is the answer to everything
- ♥ God is love, I am created in His image
- ♥ God and I are one, we belong to each other
- ♥ I am loved
- ♥ God loved me first
- ♥ I engage in random acts of kindness daily
- ♥ All works of love are works of peace
- ♥ I let love flow through me
- ♥ I extend God's love to everyone around me
- ♥ I choose to be compassionate
- ♥ Love nourishes my heart
- ♥ Jesus commands us to love and serve one another

_____
_____
_____
_____
_____

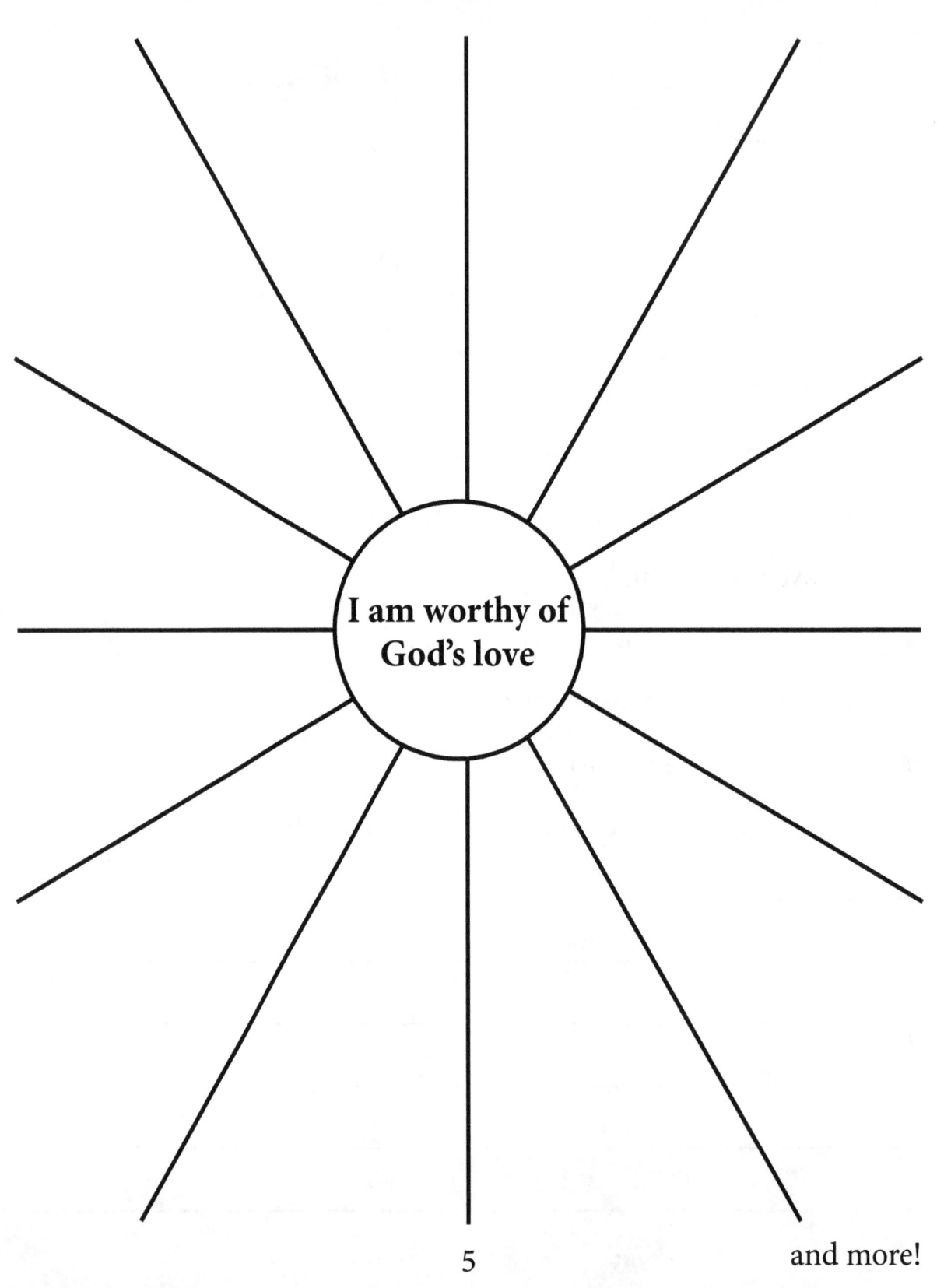

and more!

I am worthy of God's love

Variations: I am worthy and deserving, I am worthy

♥ I am a child of God, He is my father

♥ He made me exactly as I am, He made me in His perfection

♥ I know what it feels like to be worthy

♥ I am part of God's almighty plan

♥ God is love

♥ Humanity is God's chosen creation and I am human

♥ God is always with me and here for me

♥ Jesus died for me

♥ The Bible tells me that I am worthy of His love

♥ God made promises to me, promises of hope and a future

♥ I am lovable

♥ I am saved by grace

_____

_____

_____

_____

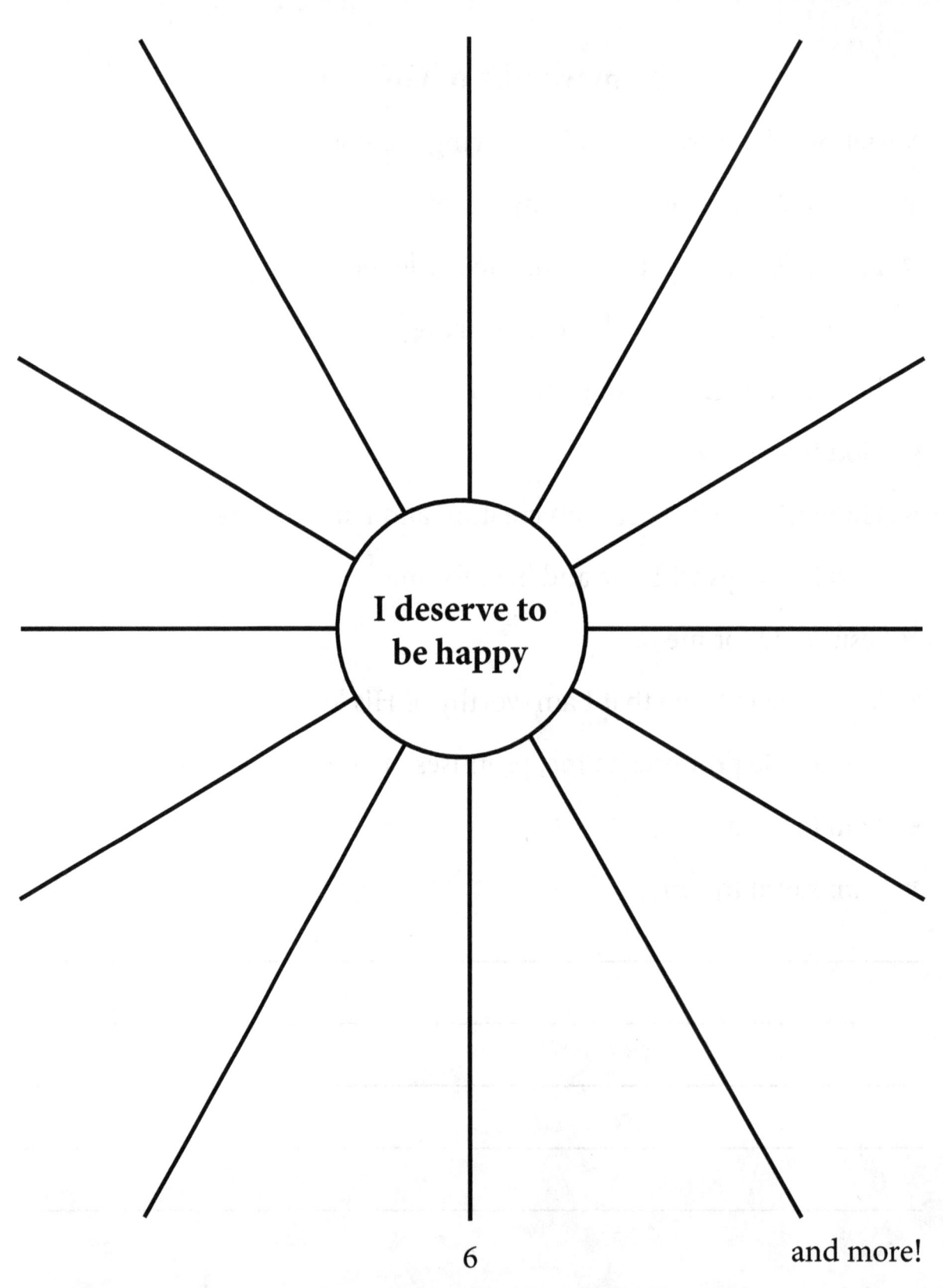

I deserve to be happy

Variations: I am full of joy, I have fun

- ♥ God loves me
- ♥ God says rejoice
- ♥ Jesus died completing a beautiful work so that I can rejoice and live in joy
- ♥ God is a high vibration and joy is a high vibration, I vibrate in a high vibration when I am happy
- ♥ Every father wishes for his child to be happy, God is my Father
- ♥ Happiness is a choice
- ♥ Happiness is free
- ♥ I have fun all the time
- ♥ I deserve everything that is good
- ♥ I am alive, I live in a free country
- ♥ I trust in God
- ♥ I choose fun every day

_____

_____

_____

_____

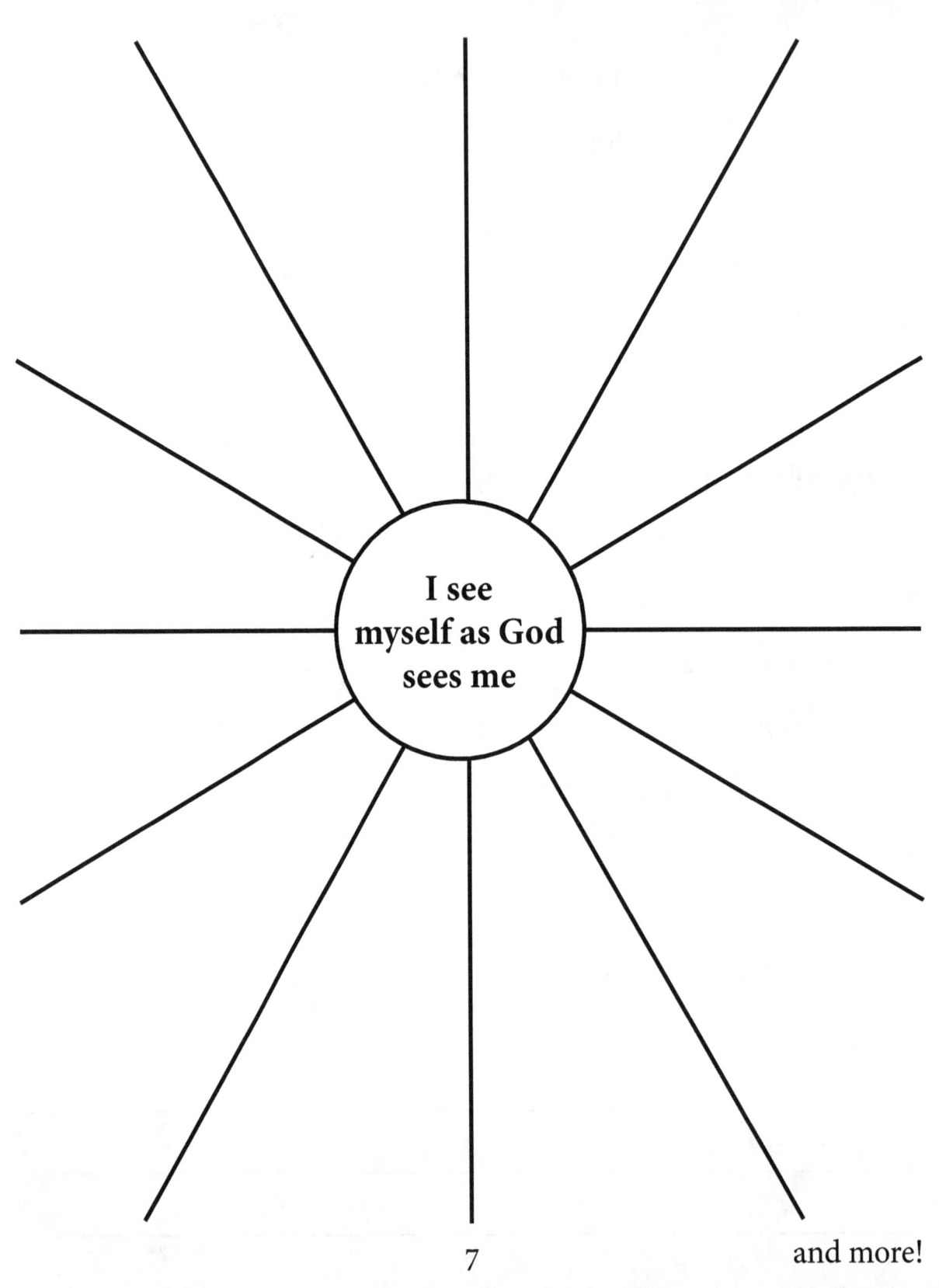

and more!

I see myself as God sees me

- ♥ I love myself
- ♥ I am a radiant being
- ♥ I am blessed by God
- ♥ I am His child
- ♥ I am perfect
- ♥ I am worthy
- ♥ I am loved
- ♥ My mind is genius
- ♥ I will inherit His Kingdom
- ♥ I am a divine being
- ♥ His Holy Spirit is in me
- ♥ God made me in His image and knows every hair on my head

_____
_____
_____
_____
_____

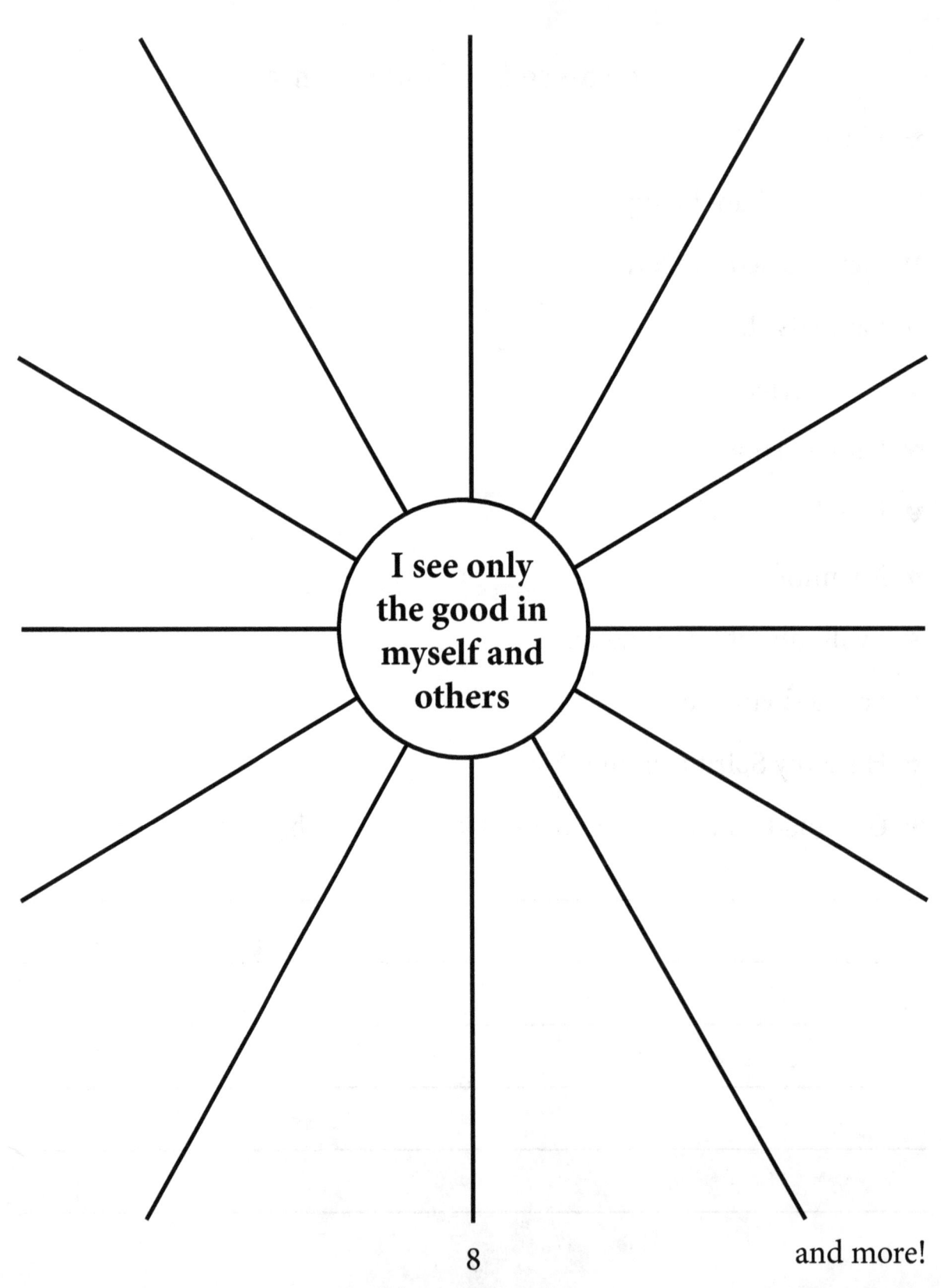

and more!

I see only the good in myself and others

- ♥ I live in love, love flows through me
- ♥ I am aligned to all the goodness in my life
- ♥ God sees me and everyone as perfect
- ♥ I see myself and others through God's eyes
- ♥ I practice forgiving, I am forever giving
- ♥ I master defensiveness
- ♥ There is always something good in everyone and in every situation
- ♥ I learn from everyone, every interaction is an opportunity to grow
- ♥ I am always learning, growing, expanding and changing for the better
- ♥ Everyone is here on Earth with a divine mission
- ♥ I appreciate the uniqueness and variety of people
- ♥ I only focus on the good

_____

_____

_____

_____

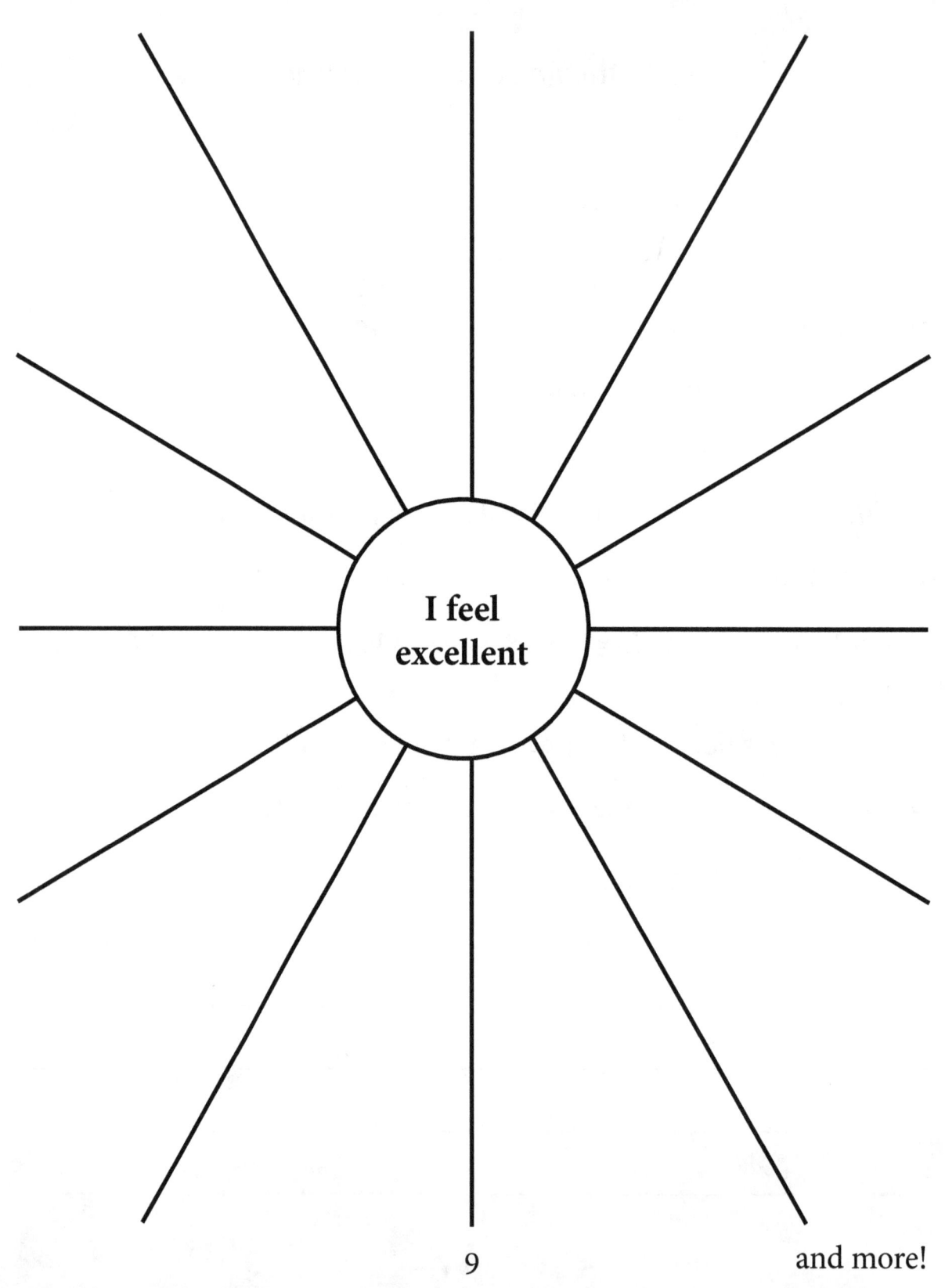

9 and more!

I feel excellent

Variation: I feel excellent about myself

- ♥ I know life is better every day
- ♥ I choose to feel excellent always
- ♥ I am grateful to be alive and thriving
- ♥ I am learning new things every day
- ♥ I take one day at a time
- ♥ I count my blessings
- ♥ God loves and prospers me
- ♥ I hold the keys to the Kingdom
- ♥ I trust in the great plans God has for me
- ♥ I go forth in certainty
- ♥ I am excellent
- ♥ I strive for excellence

_____

_____

_____

_____

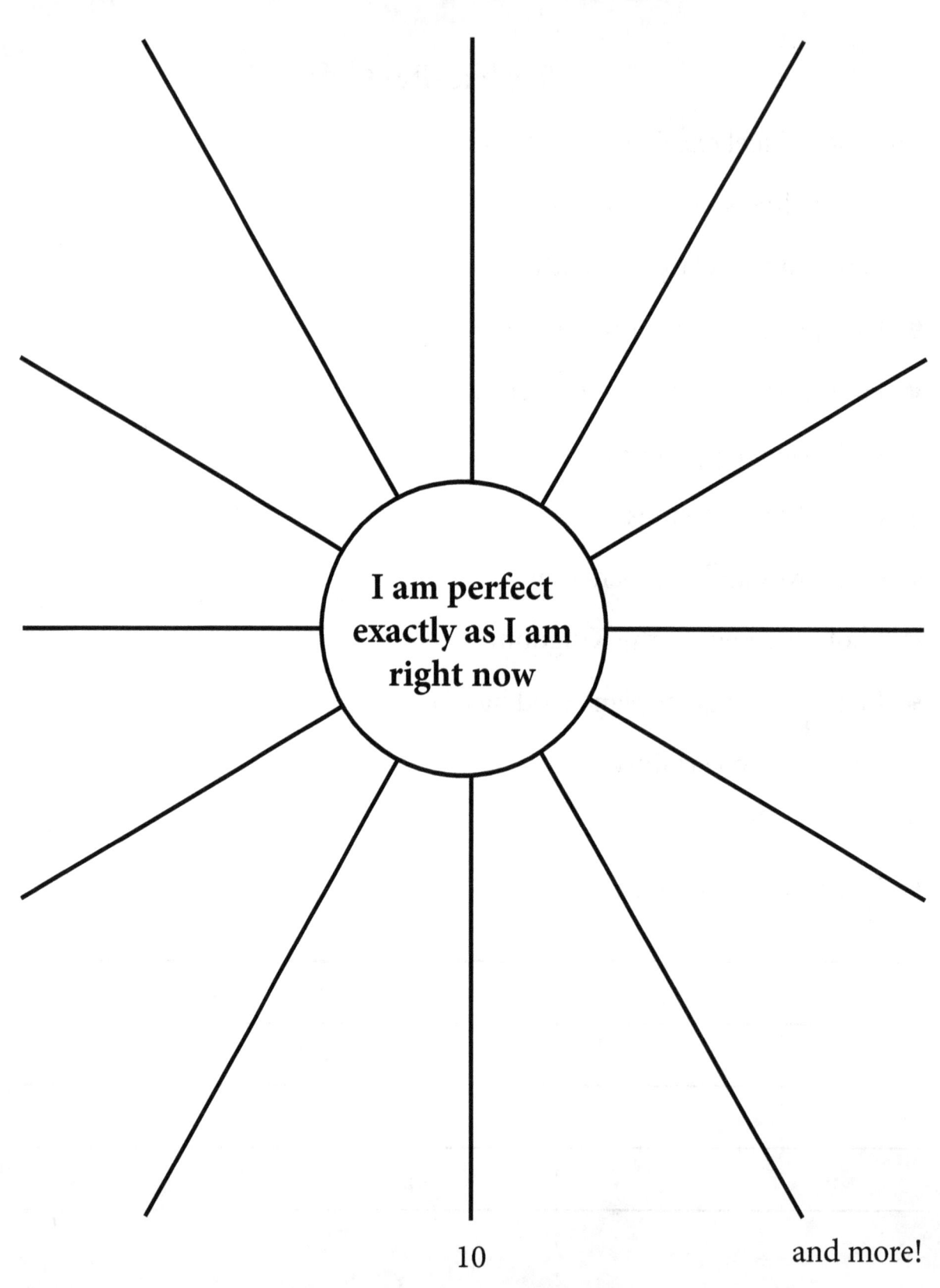

and more!

I am perfect exactly as I am right now

- ♥ God created me, He knows every hair on my head
- ♥ God sees me as perfect and I can see myself through God's eyes
- ♥ I am part of God's divine plan
- ♥ I am unique, there is only one me
- ♥ I came to fulfil my personal divine mission
- ♥ My decisions lead me to where I am right now
- ♥ God uses me as I am and where I am right now
- ♥ I trust that I have everything I require to go forth and succeed in greatness
- ♥ I am new every day
- ♥ I constantly grow, expand, and change
- ♥ God loved me first
- ♥ God chose me

_____
_____
_____
_____

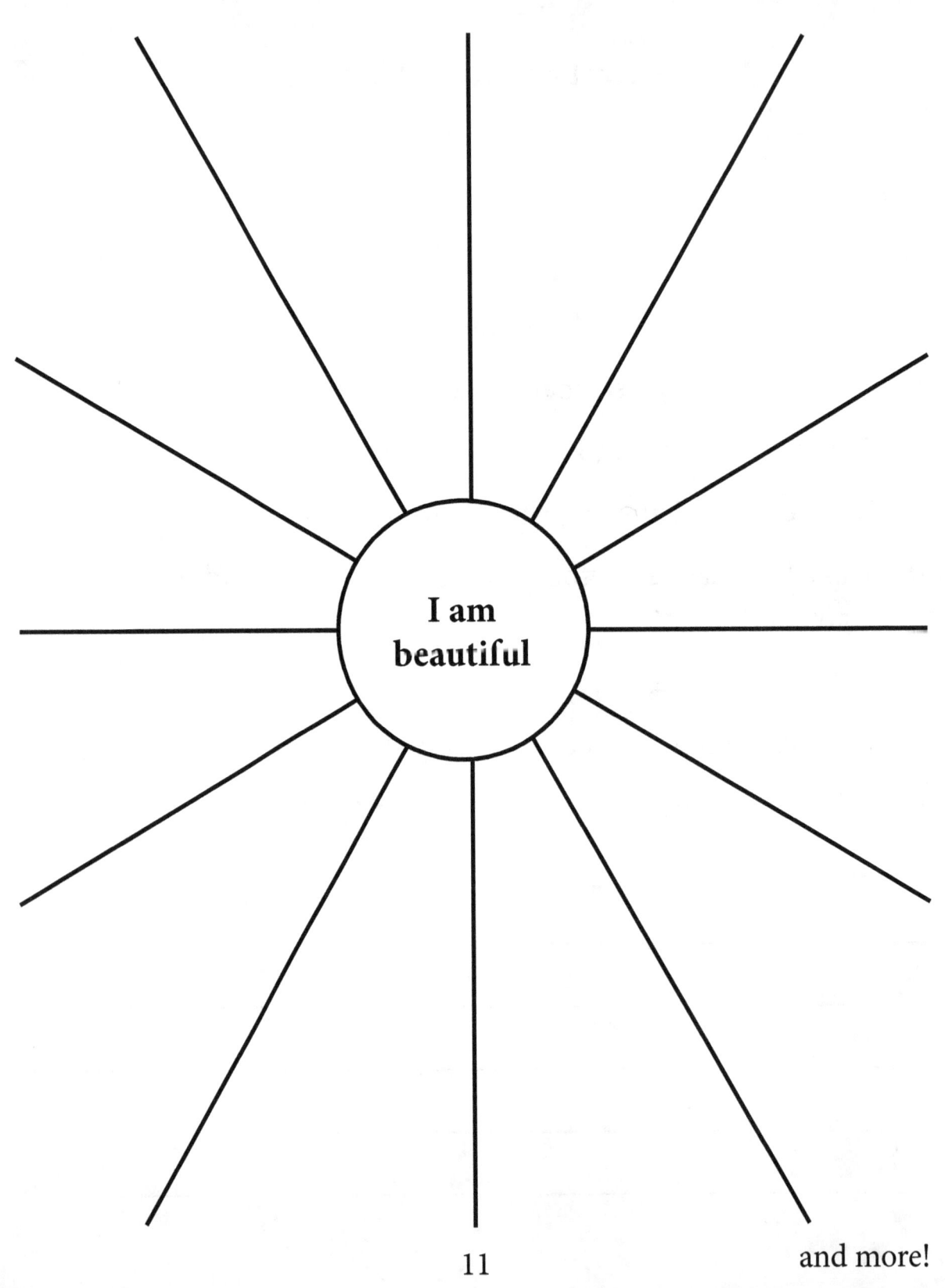

and more!

I am beautiful

Variations: Make it more personal, for example: My skin glows. I have full, thick, and healthy hair.

- ♥ I have all the body parts I require
- ♥ My best feature is _____ (my smile, my eyes, etc.)
- ♥ I have a beautiful heart
- ♥ I can change whatever I wish about my appearance
- ♥ I receive compliments about my appearance
- ♥ I see myself through God's eyes
- ♥ God made me perfect
- ♥ I am unique inside and out
- ♥ I shine with God's light
- ♥ I love to laugh
- ♥ My smile enhances my beauty
- ♥ I see the good in myself and those around me

_____

_____

_____

_____

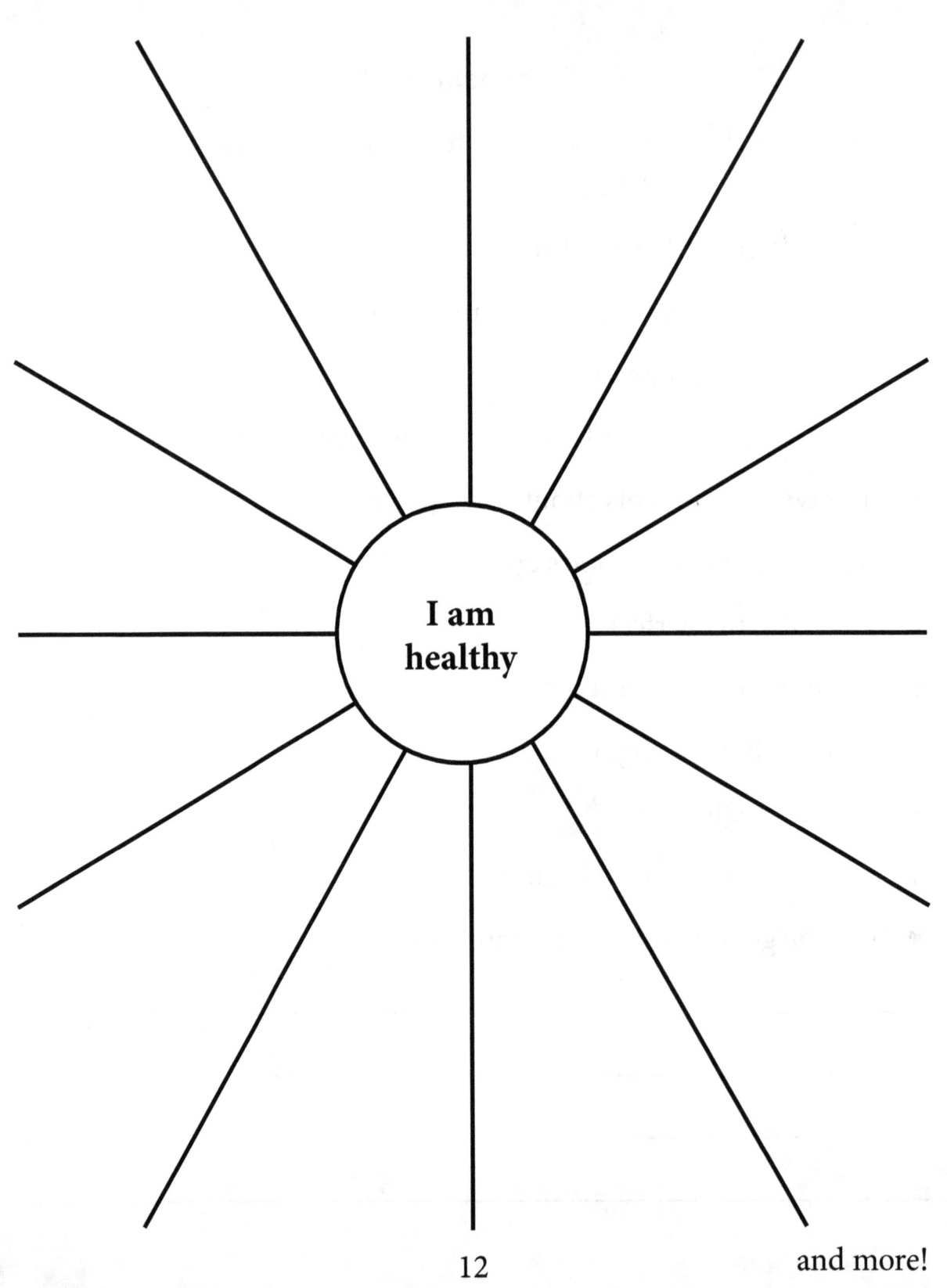

I am healthy

- ♥ God created me perfect
- ♥ I have seen miracle healings
- ♥ Food is my medicine
- ♥ I love my body
- ♥ I vibrate with faith and confidence
- ♥ Only symbiotic organisms are allowed to share my physical body with me
- ♥ I choose to set down everything that opposes my health and happiness
- ♥ God has my well-being at heart
- ♥ Healing is here
- ♥ Everything good comes from God
- ♥ I feel great and energized
- ♥ I accept my perfect health

_____

_____

_____

_____

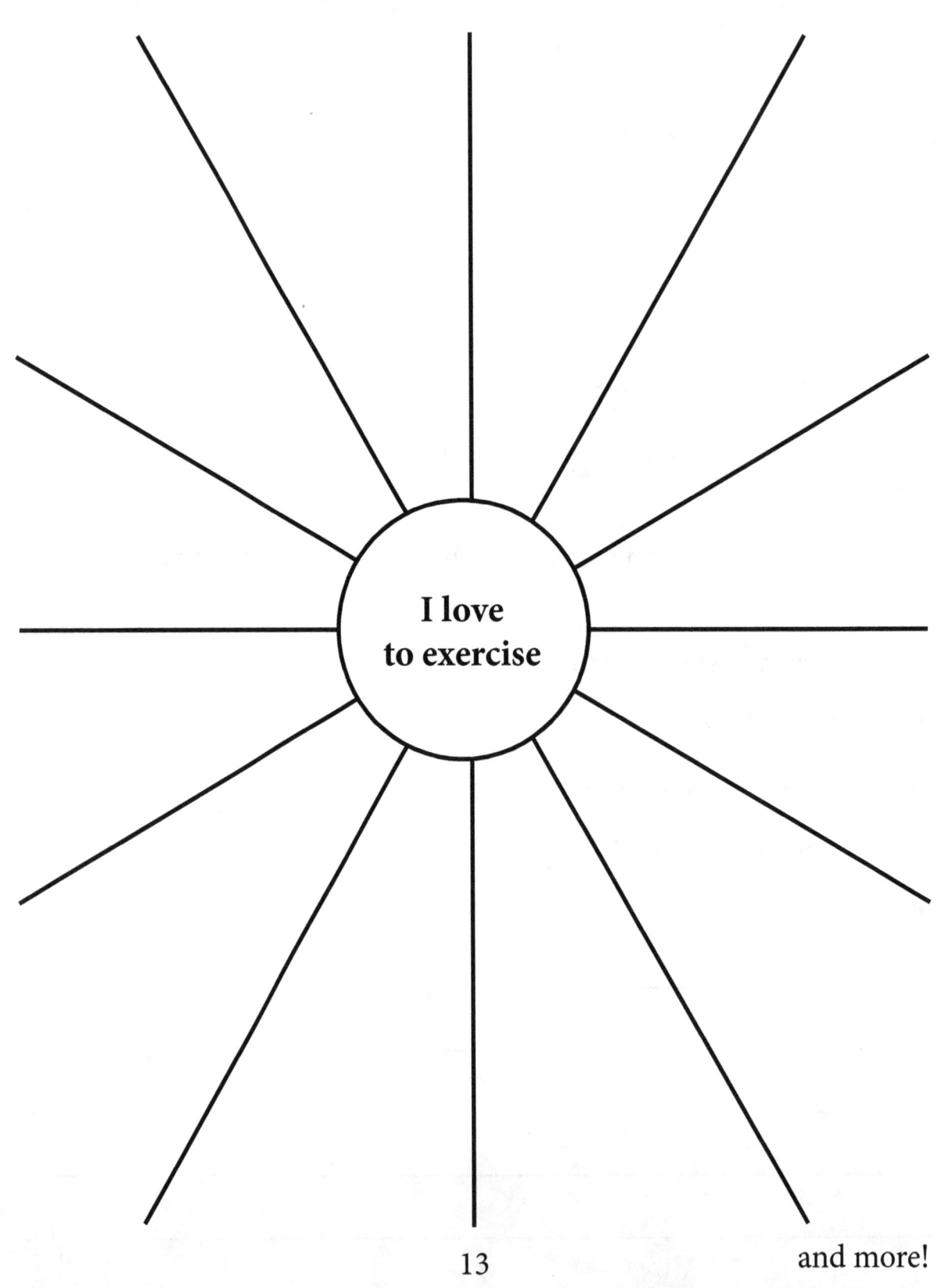

and more!

I love to exercise

- ♥ I love my body
- ♥ My body serves me well
- ♥ I know that exercise is good for me
- ♥ Exercise is healthy
- ♥ I deserve to be fit
- ♥ My body is my temple
- ♥ My fit body is part of my overall well-being
- ♥ Exercise feels good
- ♥ Whenever I exercise I feel proud of myself
- ♥ Exercise is a great way to start the day
- ♥ The time spent exercising is time spent honoring myself
- ♥ The more I exercise the more youthful I feel

_____

_____

_____

_____

_____

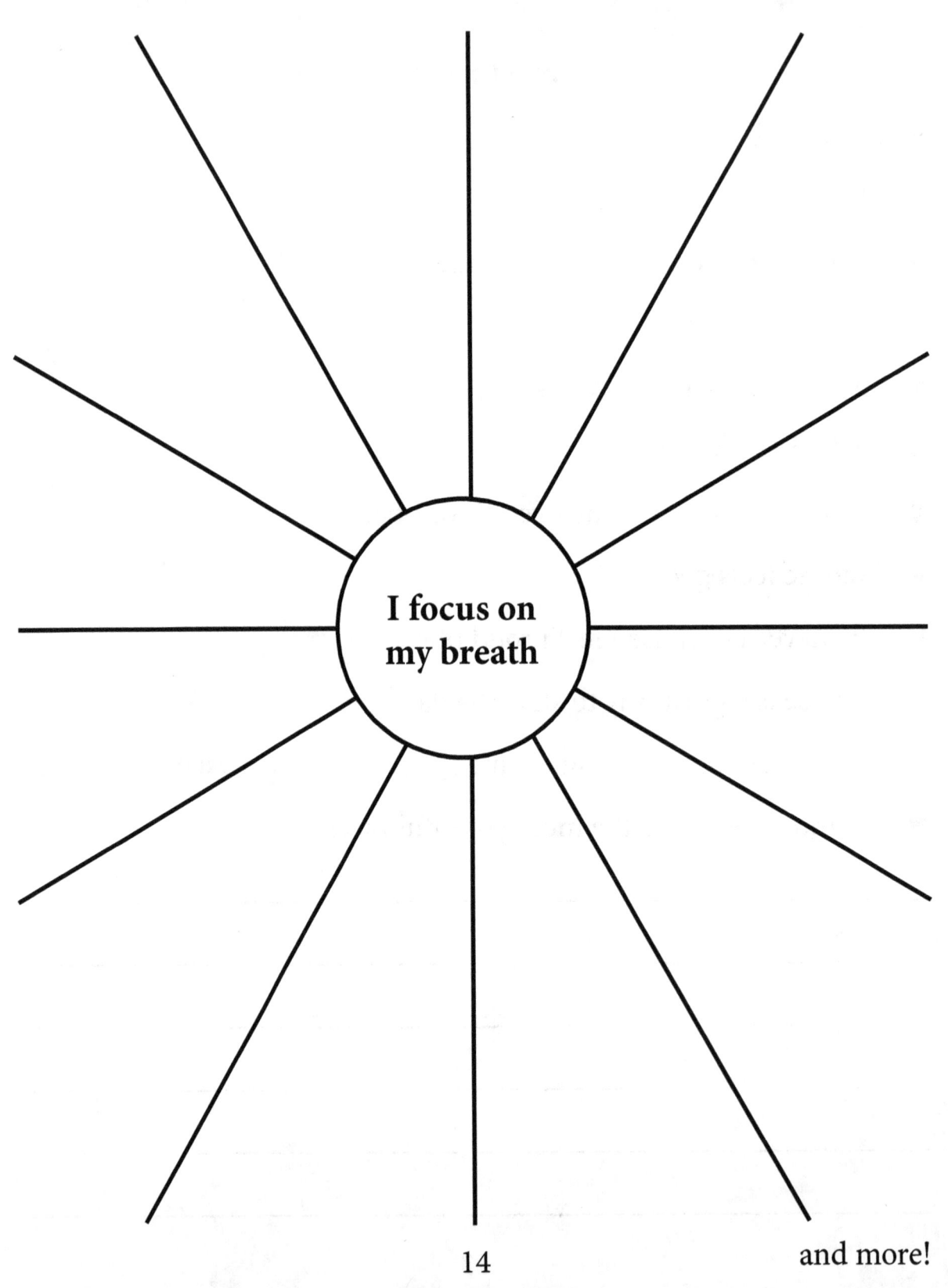

and more!

I focus on my breath

- ♥ Focusing on my breath keeps me in the present moment
- ♥ My breath of life is a gift from God
- ♥ Breathing carries oxygen to my cells
- ♥ I inhale deeply and exhale fully
- ♥ Concentrating on my breath keeps me centered
- ♥ I am calm and relaxed
- ♥ I reset myself for the next step
- ♥ My diaphragm moves and my lymph system is active while deep breathing
- ♥ My breath of life is my most precious gift
- ♥ My breath flows light and easy
- ♥ Breathing comes naturally to me
- ♥ I am alive and filled with the breath of life

_____

_____

_____

_____

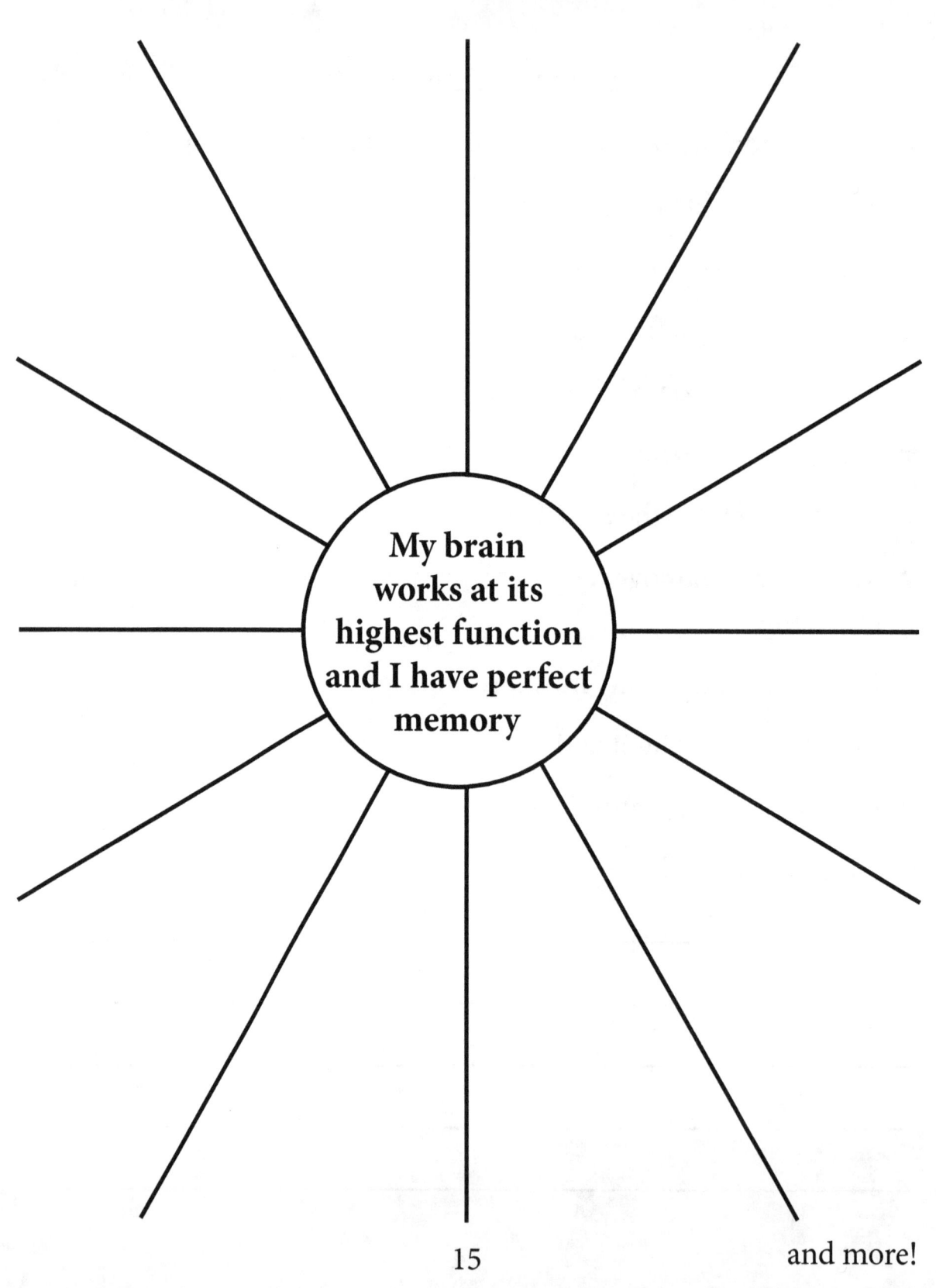

and more!

My brain works at its highest function and I have perfect memory

- ♥ I exercise my memory
- ♥ I learn a new Bible verse every day
- ♥ I challenge myself daily to remember things
- ♥ I constantly learn new things
- ♥ I balance my brain
- ♥ I breathe deeply and take in maximum oxygen
- ♥ I eat healthy food and exercise
- ♥ Essential fatty acids are part of my daily diet
- ♥ I think positive thoughts
- ♥ I correct my opposing thoughts
- ♥ I focus
- ♥ I meditate daily to clear my mind and listen to God

_____

_____

_____

_____

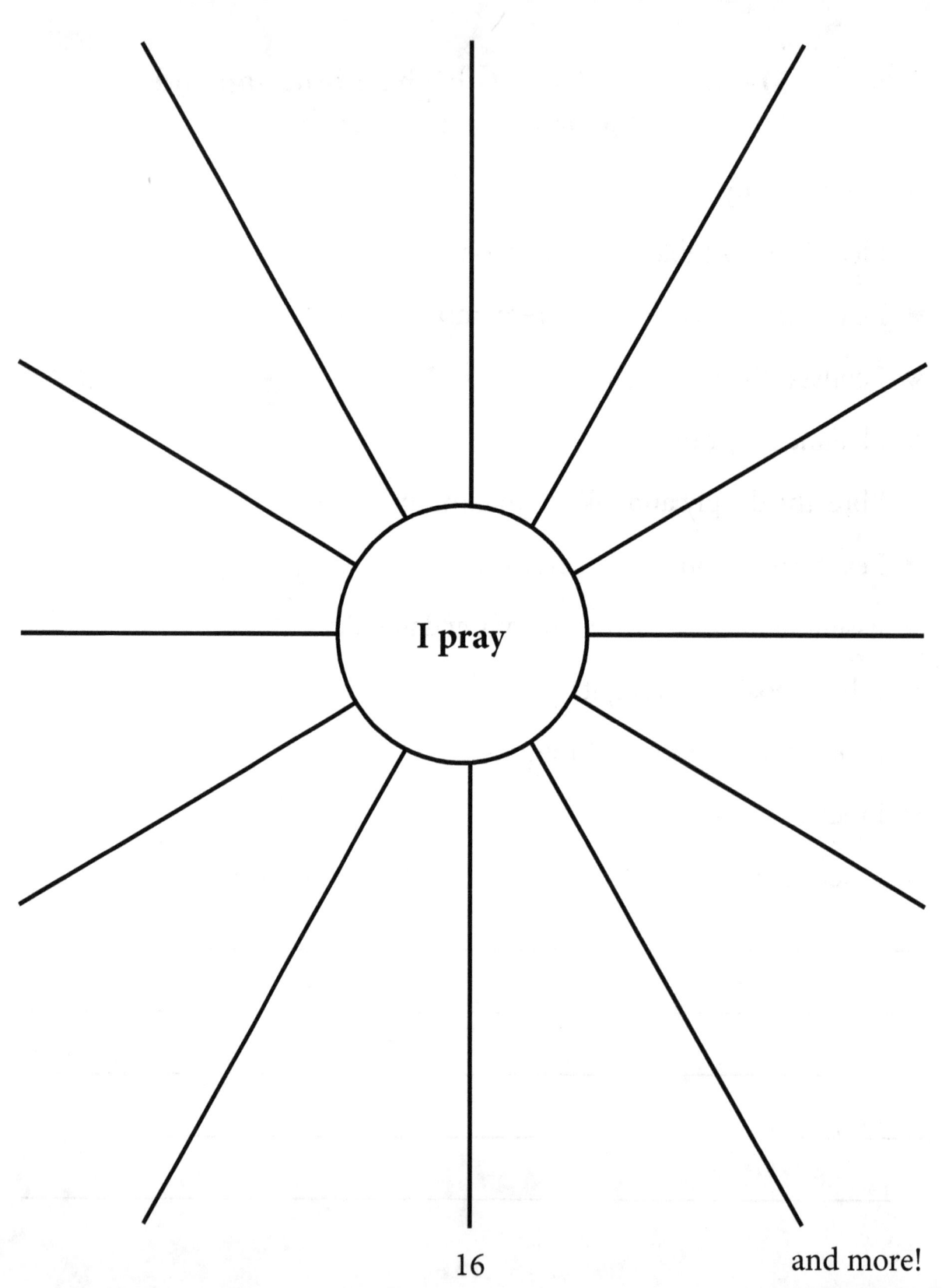

and more!

I pray

- ♥ As I pray I speak to God in conversation
- ♥ I thank God
- ♥ Prayer is casual loving communication with God
- ♥ I ask God to bless me
- ♥ I petition God for all my desires
- ♥ I call upon Jesus
- ♥ I pray with a rejoicing heart and thanksgiving
- ♥ I receive what I ask for in prayer
- ♥ God answers all prayers
- ♥ I seek Him first
- ♥ I make my heart known to God
- ♥ God is in the miracle business

_____

_____

_____

_____

_____

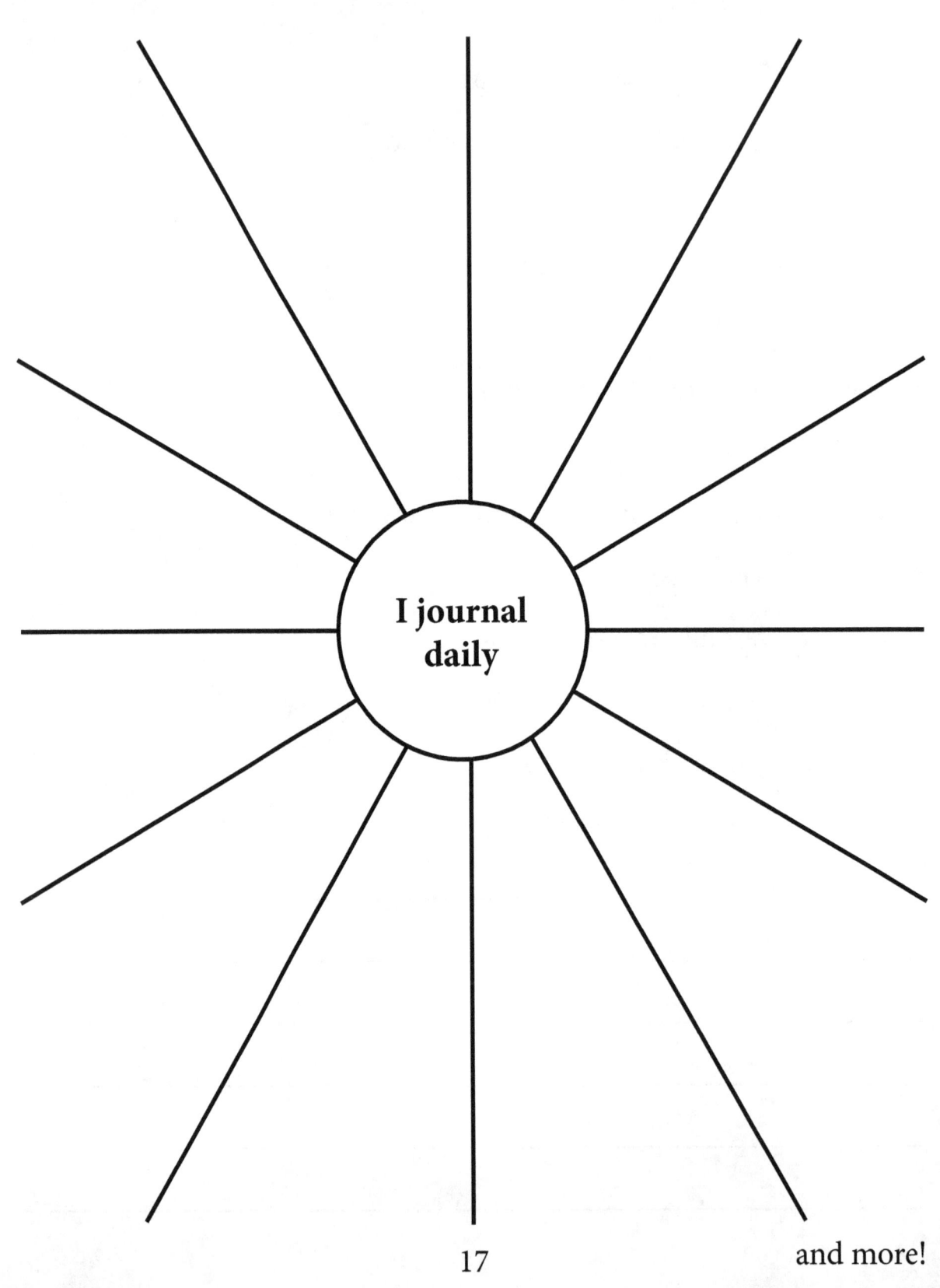

and more!

I journal daily

- ♥ I collect my thoughts on paper
- ♥ My journaled thoughts are easily edited
- ♥ My journal is the record of my life and God's miracles
- ♥ I journal my gains accomplished and miracles achieved
- ♥ I ask more to receive more
- ♥ I write down what I am grateful for each day
- ♥ I pray over my journal
- ♥ By journaling I make my heart known
- ♥ Journaling helps me to clarify my desires
- ♥ I plan my goals on paper
- ♥ I read my written pages out loud
- ♥ Journaling is a great way to gain perspective as I begin and end the day

_____

_____

_____

_____

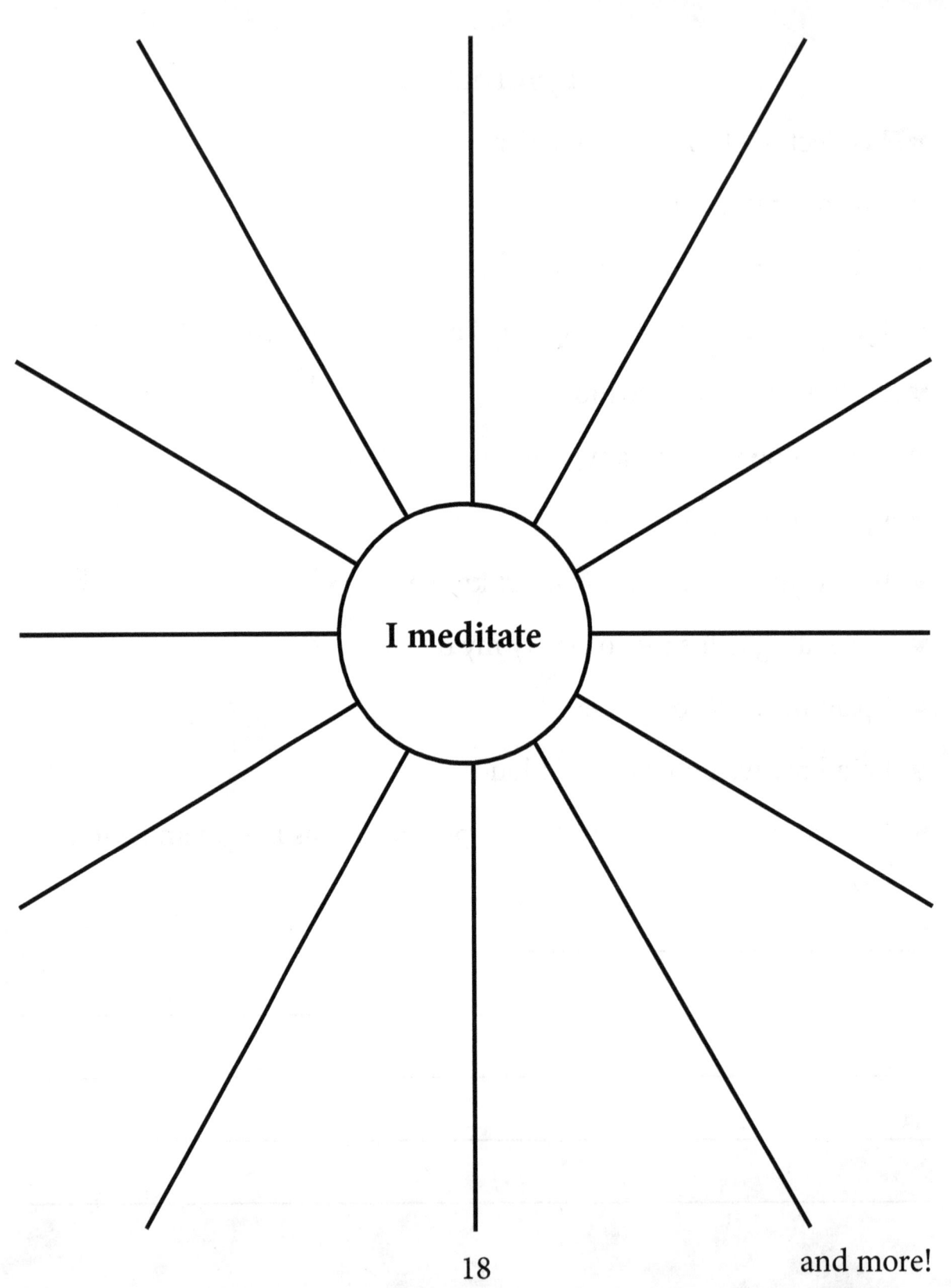

I meditate

- ♥ I welcome inspired thoughts and guidance
- ♥ Meditation is time for me
- ♥ I open my mind to receive
- ♥ I focus on my breath
- ♥ I tap into God's all-knowing and abundance
- ♥ I am balanced, relaxed, and calm
- ♥ I am connected to the light of God
- ♥ The light fills me
- ♥ I constantly create great thoughts of love and joy
- ♥ I am centered, I align my head with my heart
- ♥ I have a chosen meditation spot
- ♥ All answers flow to me as I meditate
- ♥ I listen to God

_____

_____

_____

_____

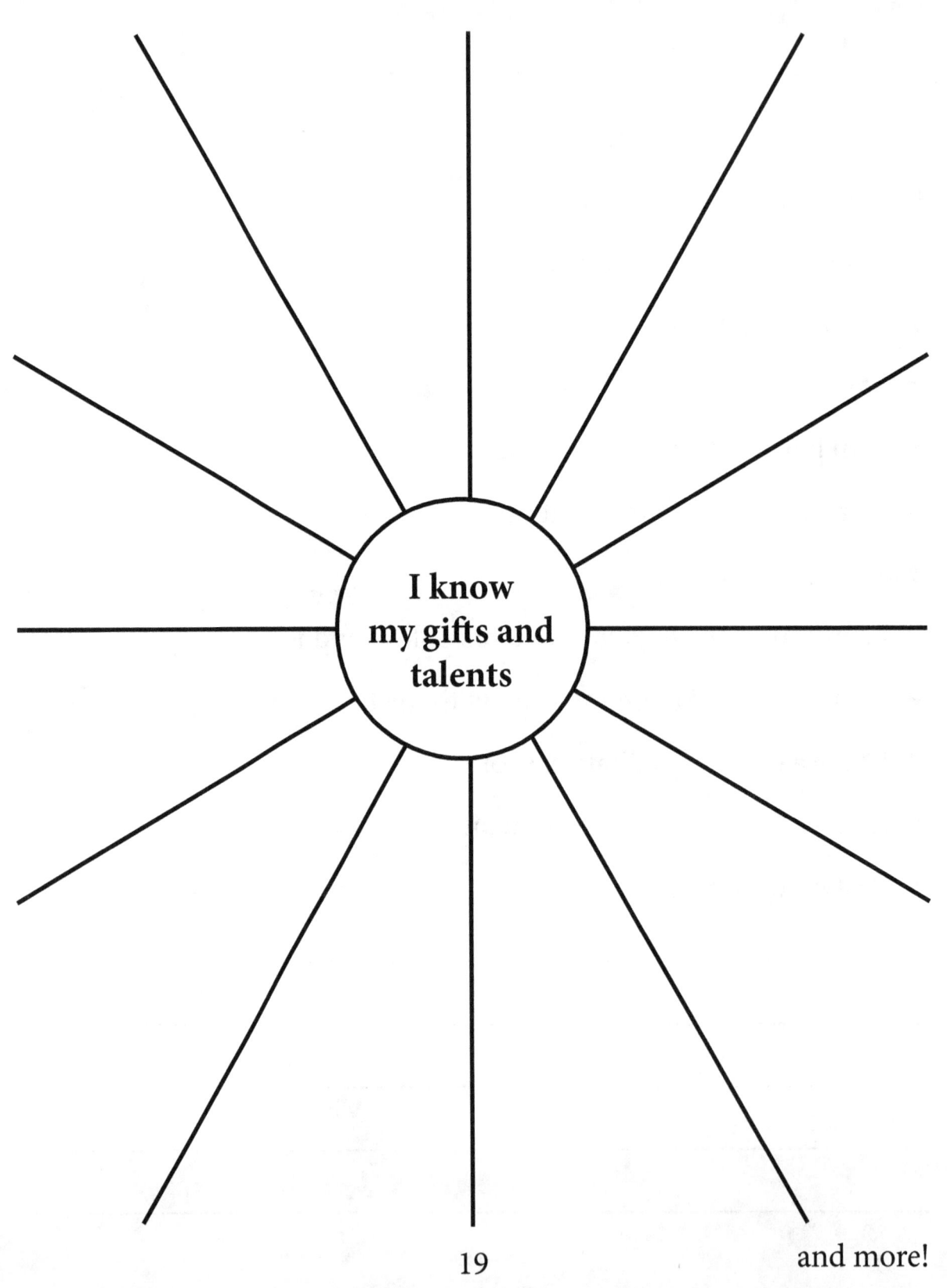

and more!

I know my gifts and talents

- ♥ I know what comes easy to me
- ♥ I pay attention to what I enjoy doing
- ♥ I know what makes my heart sing
- ♥ I can be entertained doing this all day long
- ♥ I give freely of myself
- ♥ I take inventory of myself
- ♥ I am honest with myself
- ♥ I encourage myself to do more of what I am good at
- ♥ I make a great living doing things I enjoy
- ♥ I live in joy
- ♥ My friends and family remind me of all the things I do well
- ♥ I pray to God to help me use my gifts

_____

_____

_____

_____

_____

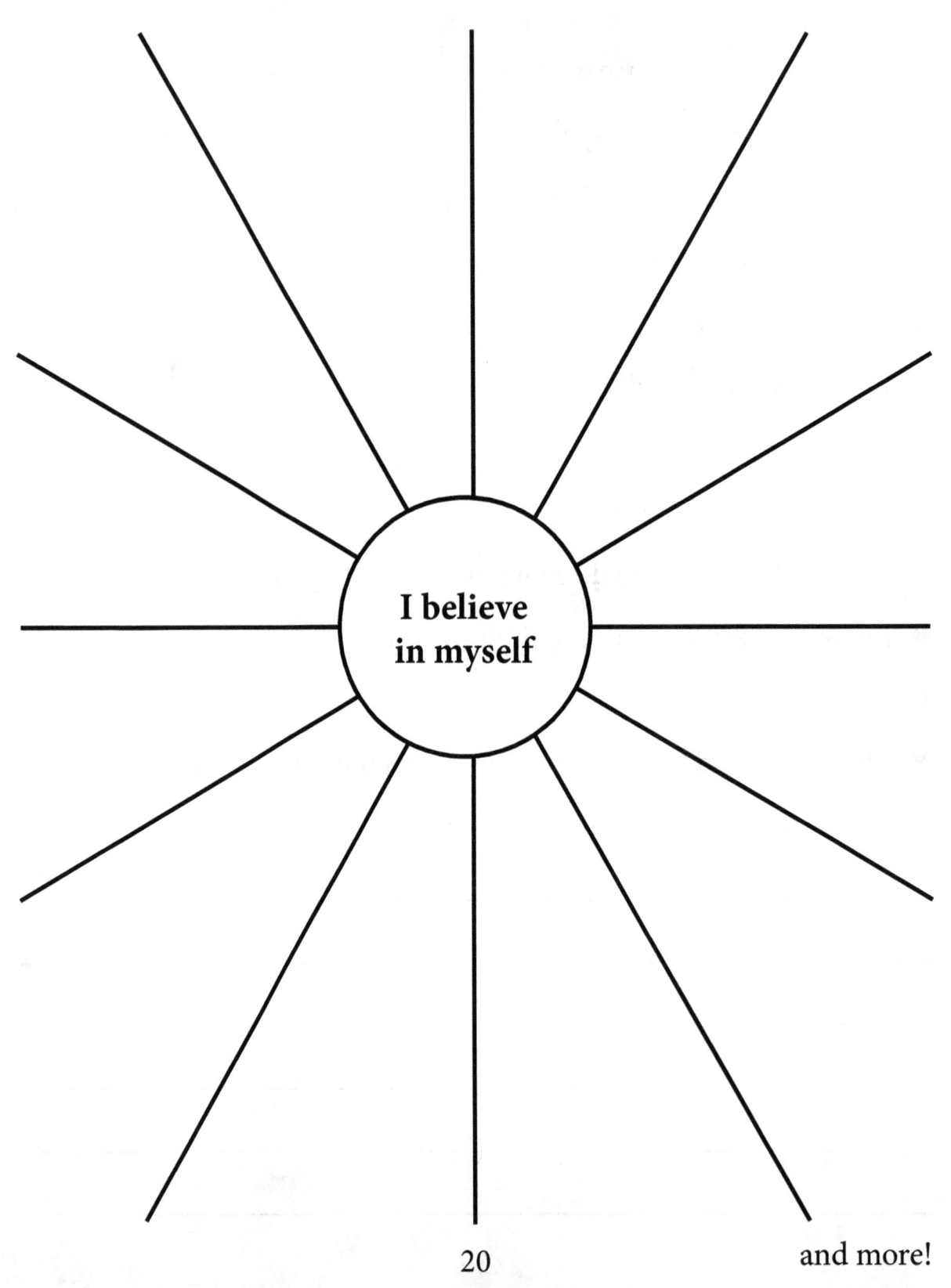

I believe in myself

- ♥ I believe that I am awesome
- ♥ I believe God wishes for me to succeed
- ♥ I am educated, intelligent, and smart
- ♥ God gave me unique gifts and talents
- ♥ I am chosen by God
- ♥ I am capable of great things
- ♥ I did it before so I can do it again
- ♥ I can figure out everything presented to me
- ♥ I can do it
- ♥ It only gets better
- ♥ I succeed in everything I do
- ♥ Every day I wake up is a win

_____

_____

_____

_____

_____

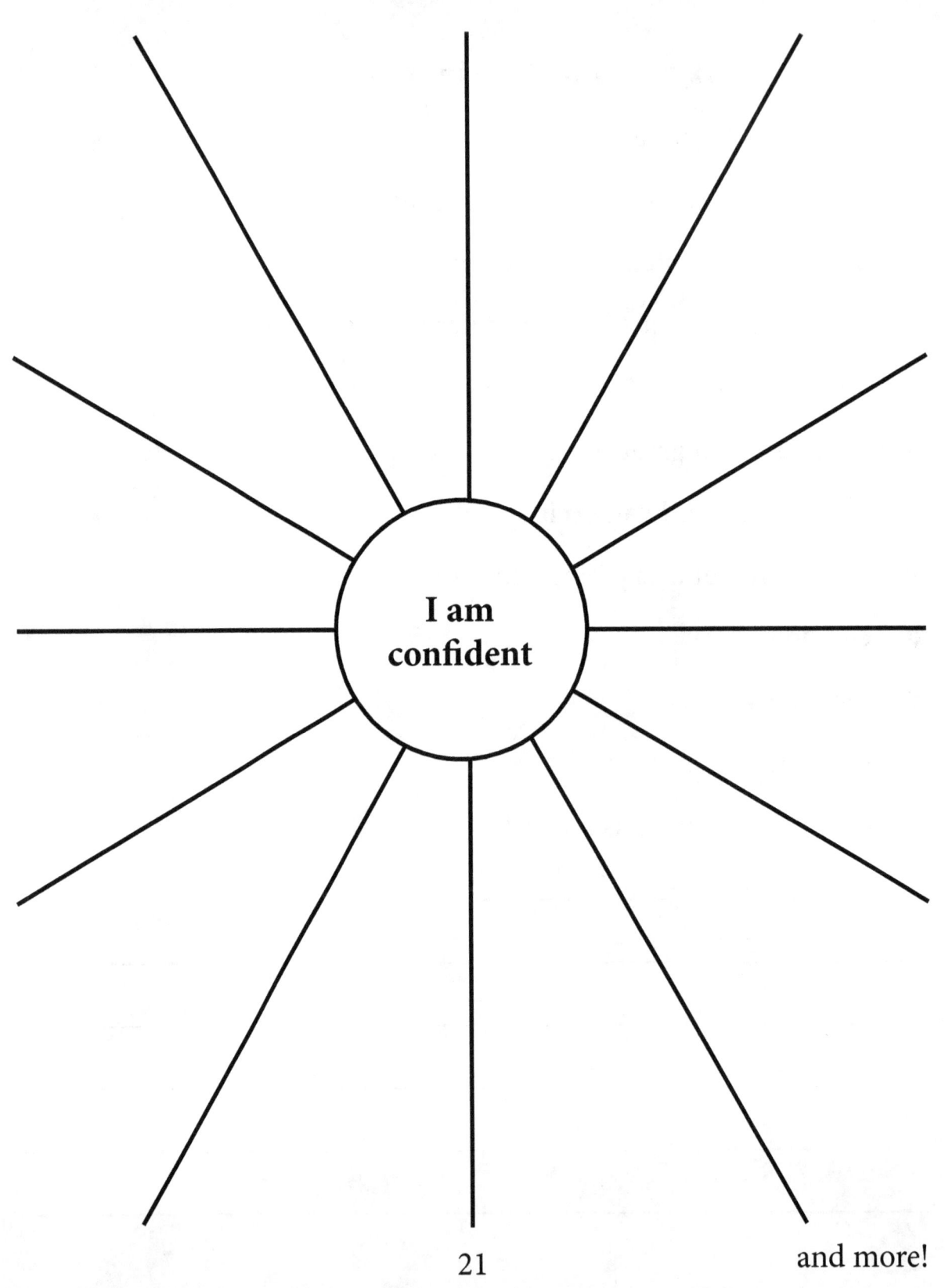

and more!

I am confident

- ♥ God is with me
- ♥ I am able
- ♥ I am willing
- ♥ I am brilliant and smart
- ♥ I am amazing
- ♥ I know how to earn money
- ♥ The Bible is full of confident role models
- ♥ I am educated
- ♥ Everything always turns out good for me
- ♥ I speak English
- ♥ God uses me for His great plan
- ♥ Everything that I require comes to me

_____

_____

_____

_____

_____

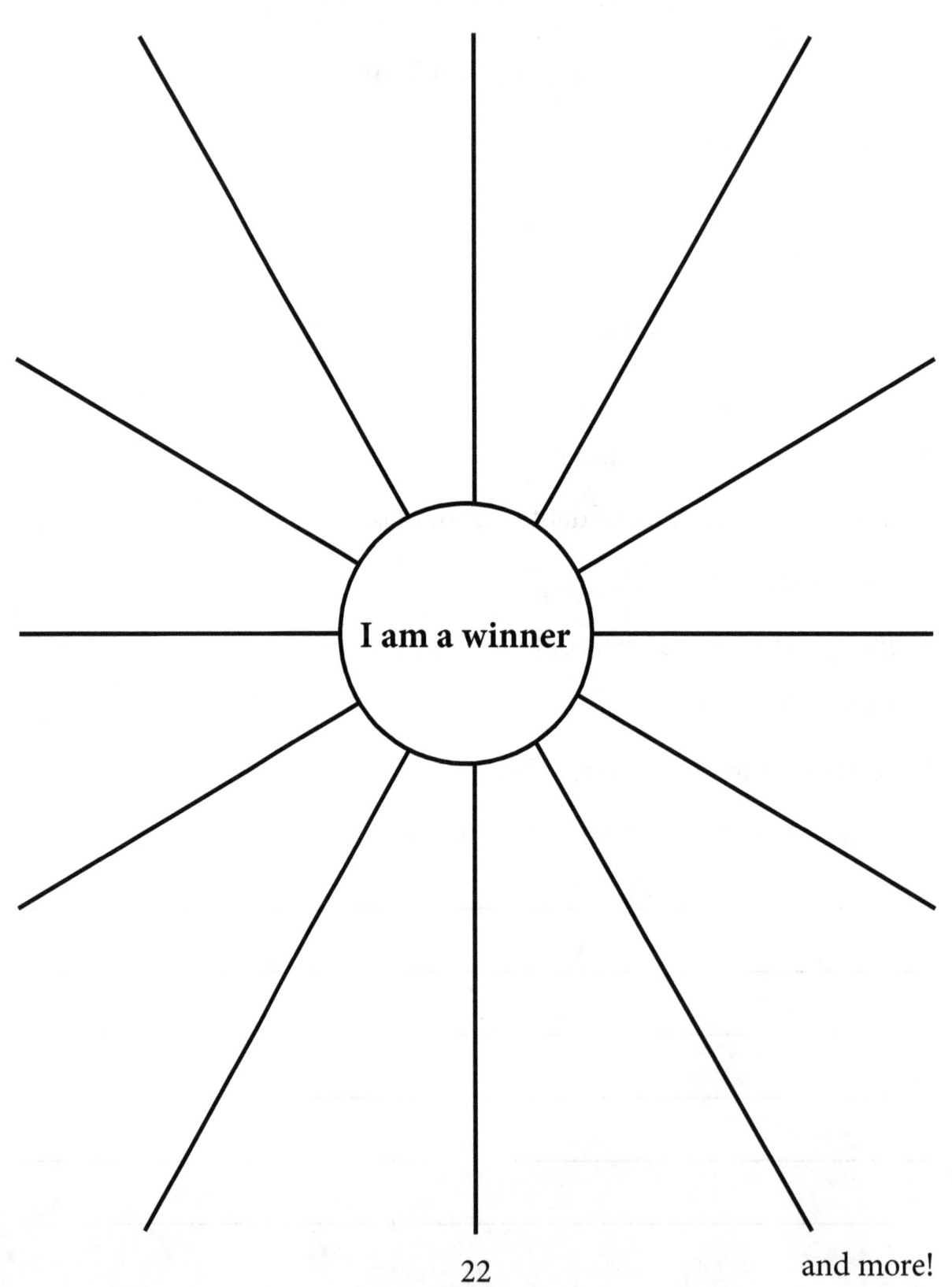

I am a winner

- ♥ God set up this Universe for me to win
- ♥ I have a solution-oriented attitude
- ♥ God desires for me to prosper
- ♥ I deserve to have it all
- ♥ I love my abundant life
- ♥ I feel good achieving
- ♥ Money gives me options
- ♥ I am worth it
- ♥ I receive continually
- ♥ I am a winner in God's world every day
- ♥ We are all winners
- ♥ Every day I am alive is a win

_____

_____

_____

_____

_____

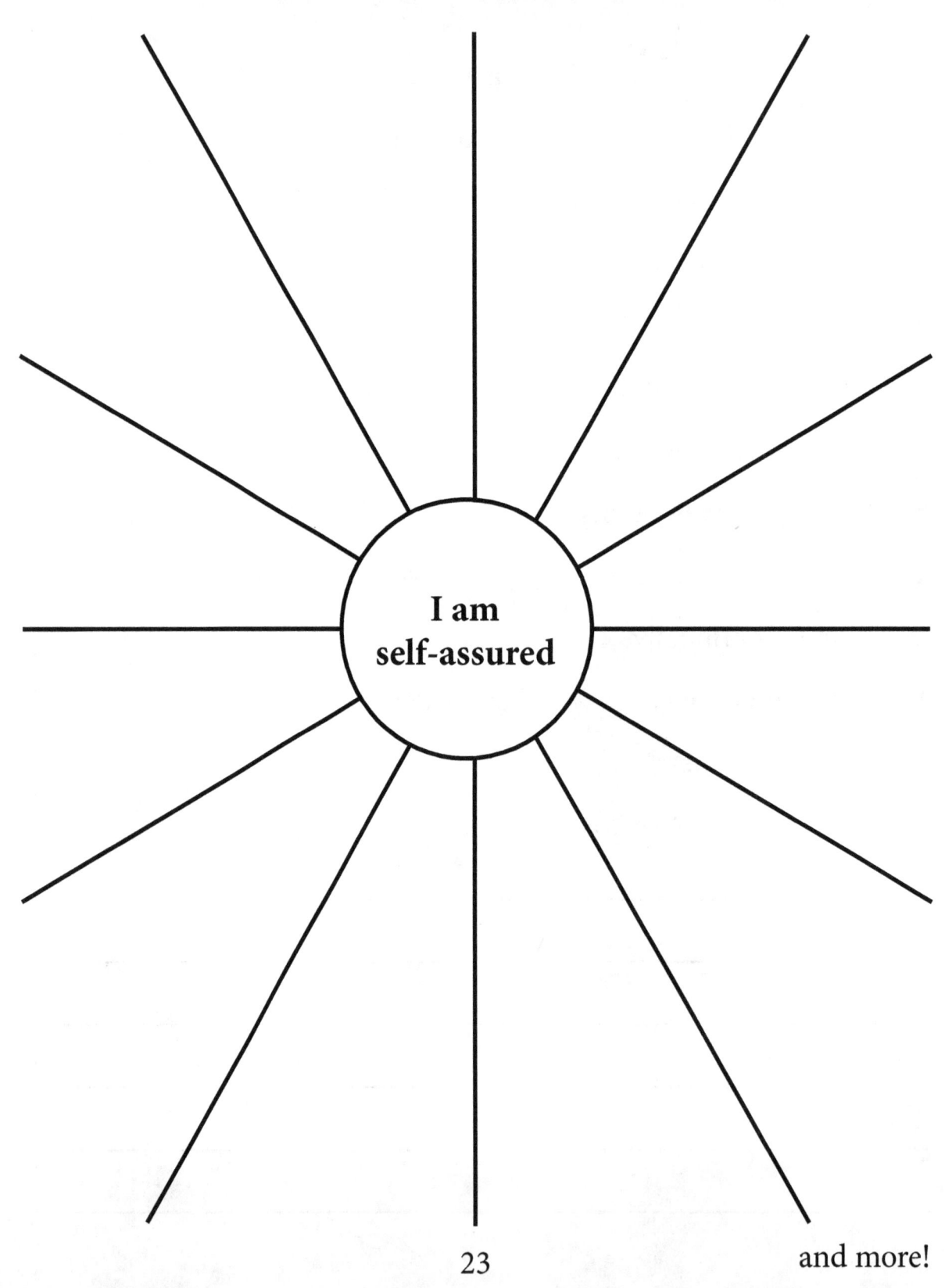

23 and more!

I am self-assured

- ♥ I live confidently with God in me, around me, and through me
- ♥ God loves me exactly as I am
- ♥ I am a good person
- ♥ I love myself and others
- ♥ I am in control of my thoughts and words
- ♥ I have the power to turn away all opposing and tempting thoughts
- ♥ I always have more than enough and I give generously
- ♥ I smile often and people enjoy my smiles and friendly words
- ♥ I understand the power of my words
- ♥ I declare my outcomes with great detail
- ♥ I live by design
- ♥ I pray first before I take action

_____

_____

_____

_____

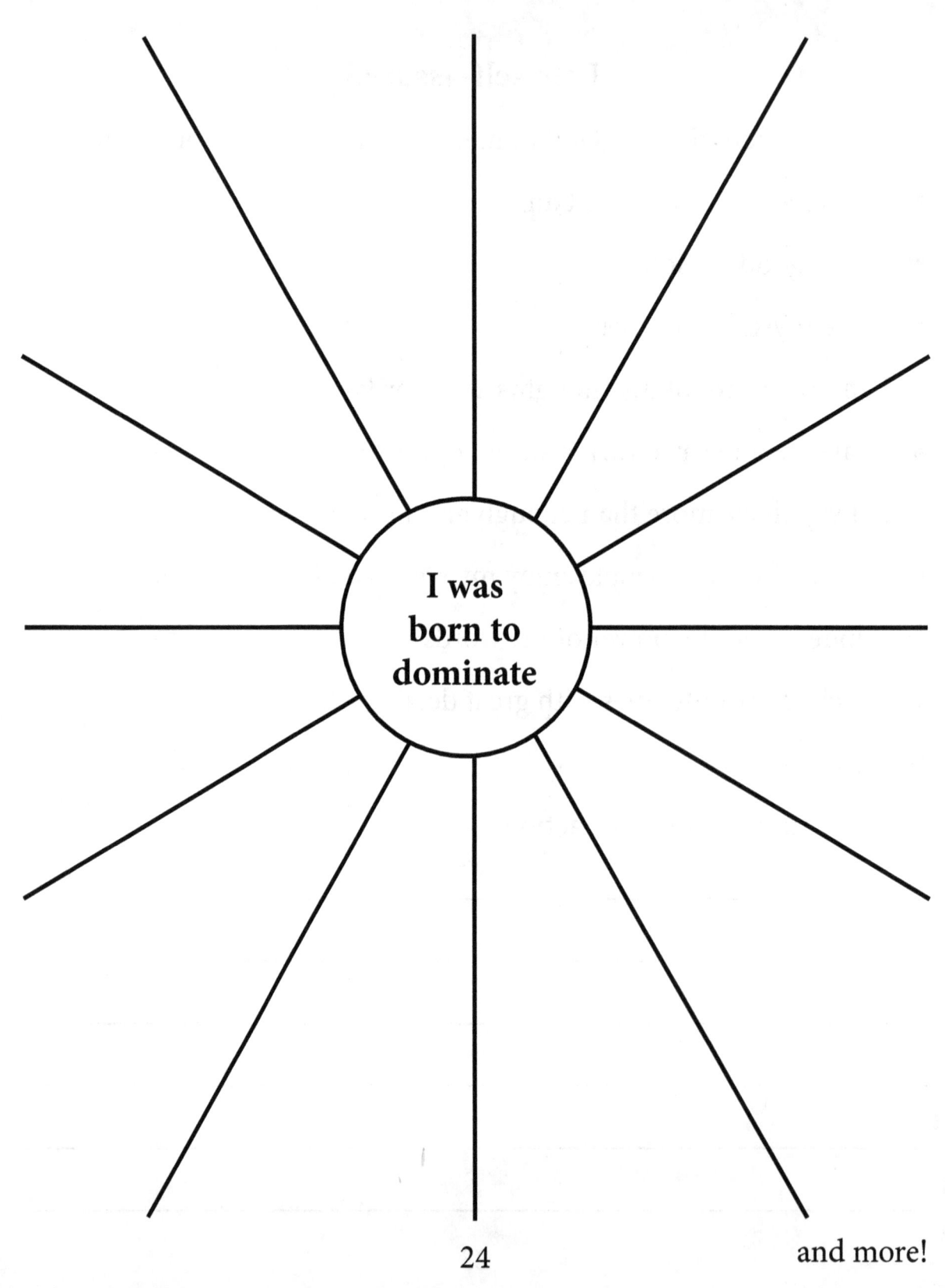

and more!

I was born to dominate

- ♥ I walk in my spiritual inheritance
- ♥ I am a child of God
- ♥ I hold the keys to the Kingdom
- ♥ God granted me dominion over the Earth
- ♥ God had Adam name all the animals to co-create with Him
- ♥ I co-create with God
- ♥ I am created to win
- ♥ I deserve the feelings of triumph, success, and accomplishment
- ♥ I start and finish at my best
- ♥ I have the power to welcome only the thoughts that bless me
- ♥ I have the power to turn away all opposing thoughts
- ♥ I love the feelings of accomplishment and victory

_____

_____

_____

_____

_____

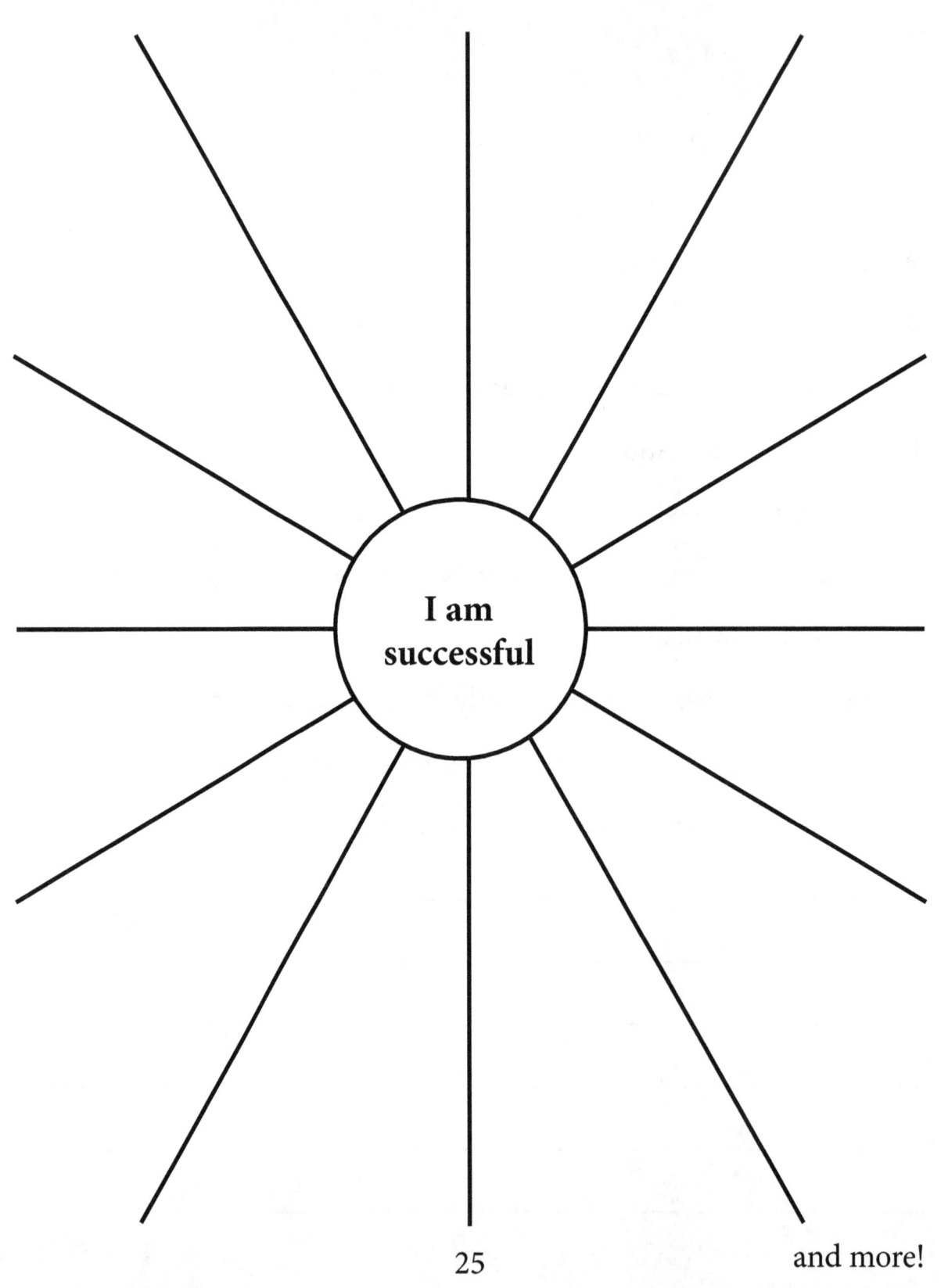

I am successful

- ♥ I feel fulfilled
- ♥ I am educated
- ♥ I am balanced and at peace
- ♥ I have unique talents and gifts
- ♥ I attract abundance
- ♥ I love myself and others
- ♥ I attract great relationships and partners
- ♥ I do what I am great at
- ♥ Business flows easy to me
- ♥ I am blessed by God
- ♥ I play on God's team
- ♥ I welcome new opportunities

_____

_____

_____

_____

_____

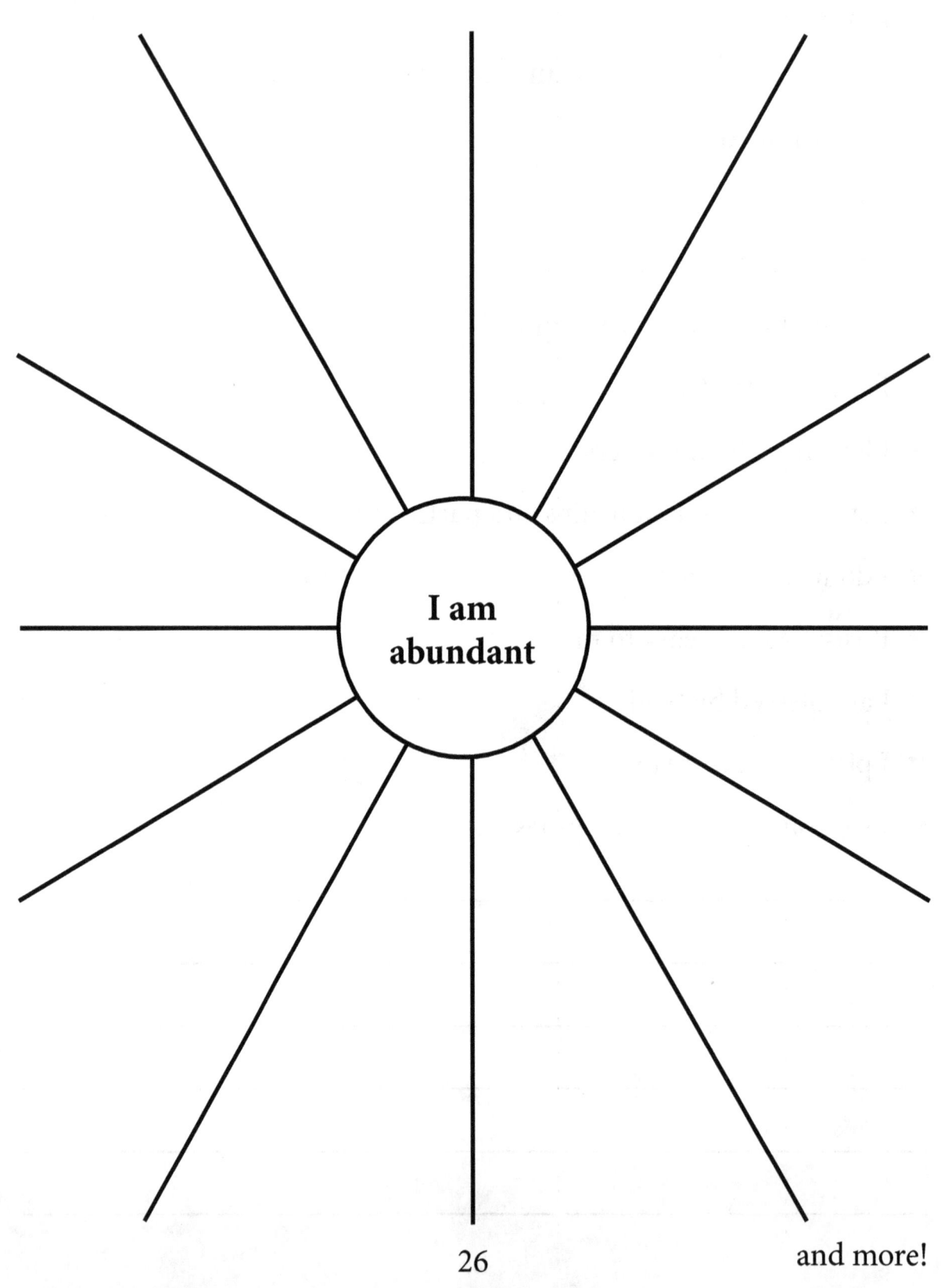

I am abundant

Variations: I now joyfully accept and appreciate the abundant life the Universe offers me, My perfect life is full of abundance, I recognize abundance everywhere, I tap into all the abundance

- ♥ I give a portion of everything I receive
- ♥ Money flows light and easy to me
- ♥ I handle money well
- ♥ I have an abundant mindset
- ♥ Wealth comes to me from everywhere
- ♥ Everything wonderful finds its way to me
- ♥ I believe in abundance
- ♥ God is an abundant God
- ♥ God owns everything and He loves to share
- ♥ God has so much to give and I receive continually
- ♥ There will always be more
- ♥ I think thoughts and speak words of abundance

_____

_____

_____

_____

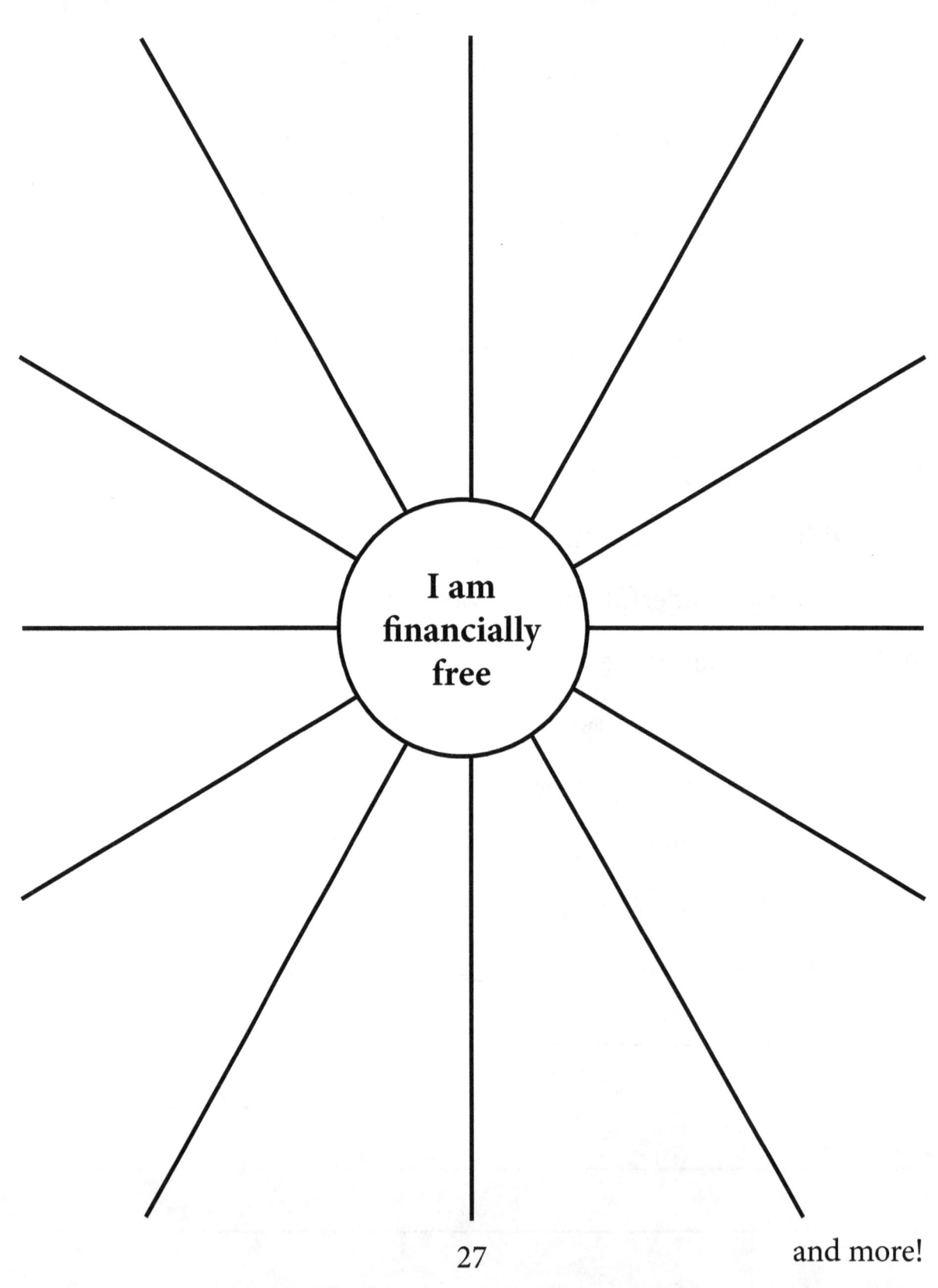

and more!

I am financially free

- ♥ Having money and watching it grow is fun
- ♥ I am smart and educated, I can read and write, I have life experience
- ♥ God owns everything
- ♥ I am a cheerful giver, it feels amazing to pay it forward, it is fun to pay it forward
- ♥ I am a talented _____
- ♥ I have the discipline within me to carry out my plans with God's help
- ♥ God can use me and having money is helpful
- ♥ I receive the help I require to create wealth in my life
- ♥ God put me on this Earth to prosper and grow
- ♥ God's in charge of all my security and He provides my abundant supply
- ♥ Money flows freely, light, and easy
- ♥ Money comes to me in various and multiple ways, money comes in many forms

_____

_____

_____

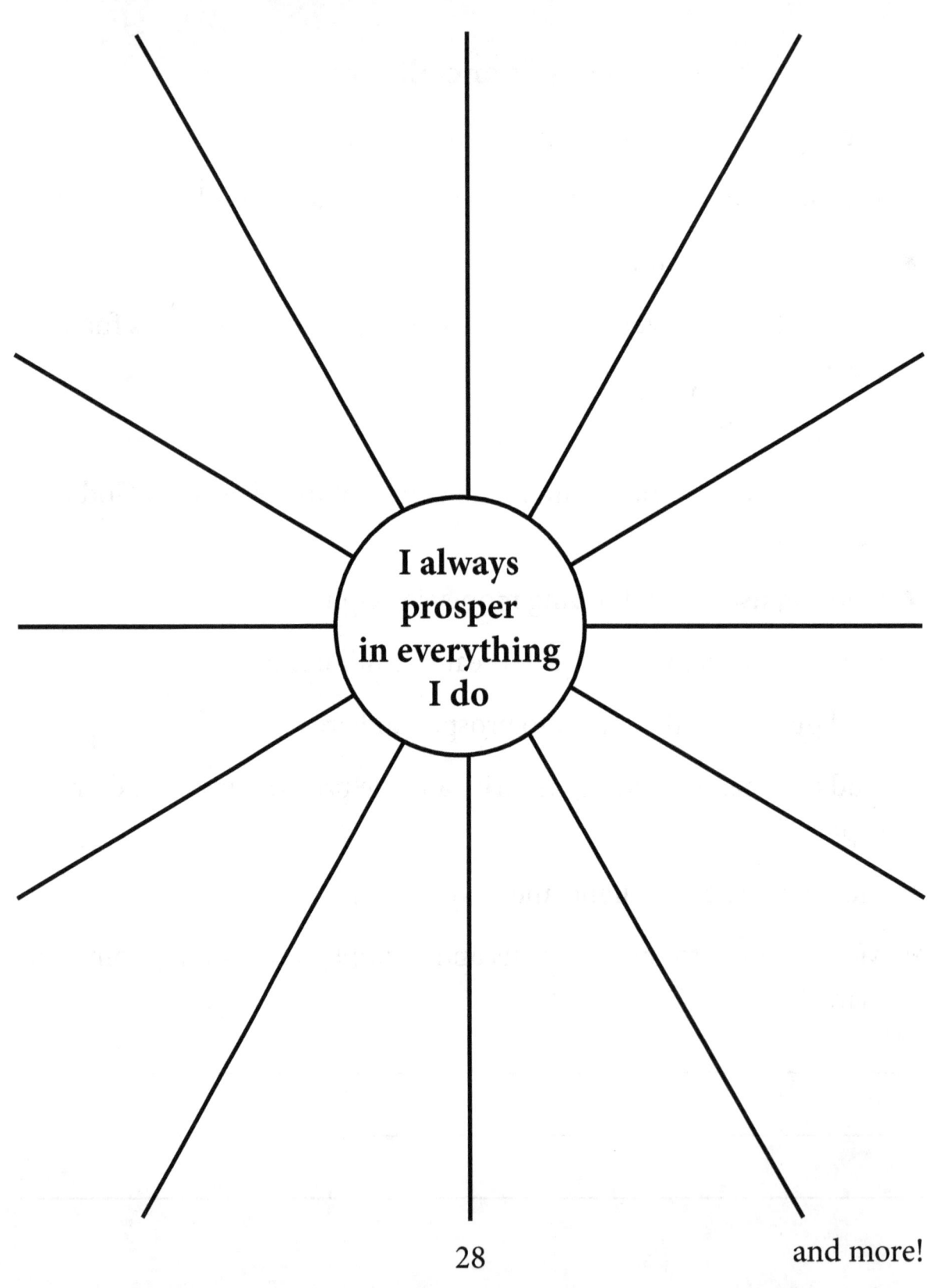

and more!

I always prosper in everything I do

- ♥ I believe in myself
- ♥ Money excites me, I enjoy earning money
- ♥ I have unique gifts and talents that help me prosper
- ♥ I have confidence
- ♥ God made me perfect and complete
- ♥ I set goals
- ♥ I live by design, I co-create with God, and write my goals down
- ♥ I believe in prosperity
- ♥ God is a prosperous God
- ♥ Everything comes easy to me
- ♥ I have my eyes on the victory
- ♥ I am a winner

_____

_____

_____

_____

_____

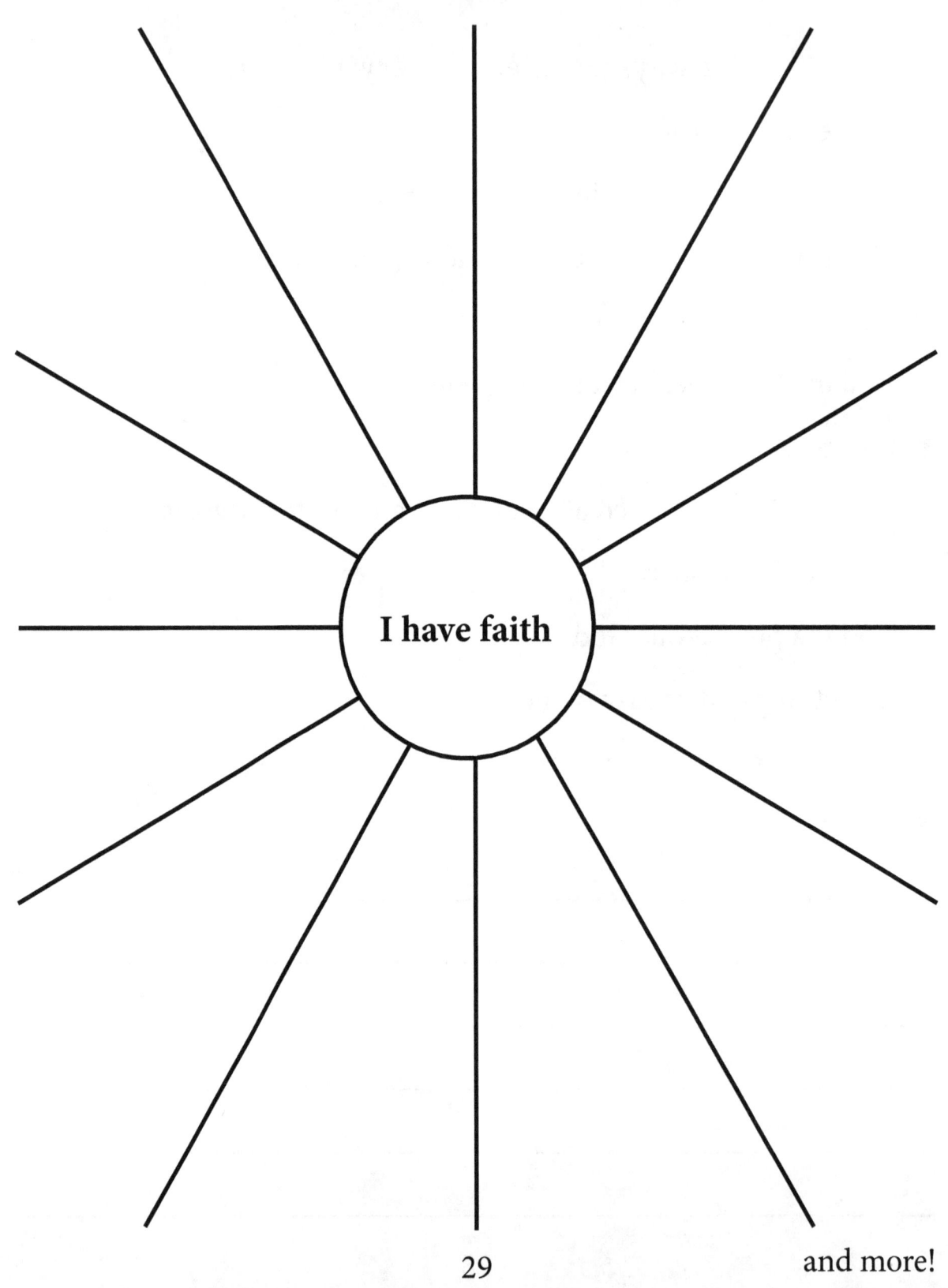

and more!

I have faith

- ♥ I am strong, I have God's garment of light around me
- ♥ I believe in God's blessings
- ♥ Jesus died for me, He did a complete work on the cross
- ♥ Everything is possible all the time
- ♥ We are miracle makers
- ♥ Jesus promised me that I can do great works
- ♥ Faith as small as a mustard seed can move mountains
- ♥ God is in me and around me, He left me with His Holy Spirit
- ♥ Life is light and easy with faith
- ♥ My faith sets me free
- ♥ My faith is my foundation and the key to my success
- ♥ Faith is one of the highest frequencies

_____

_____

_____

_____

_____

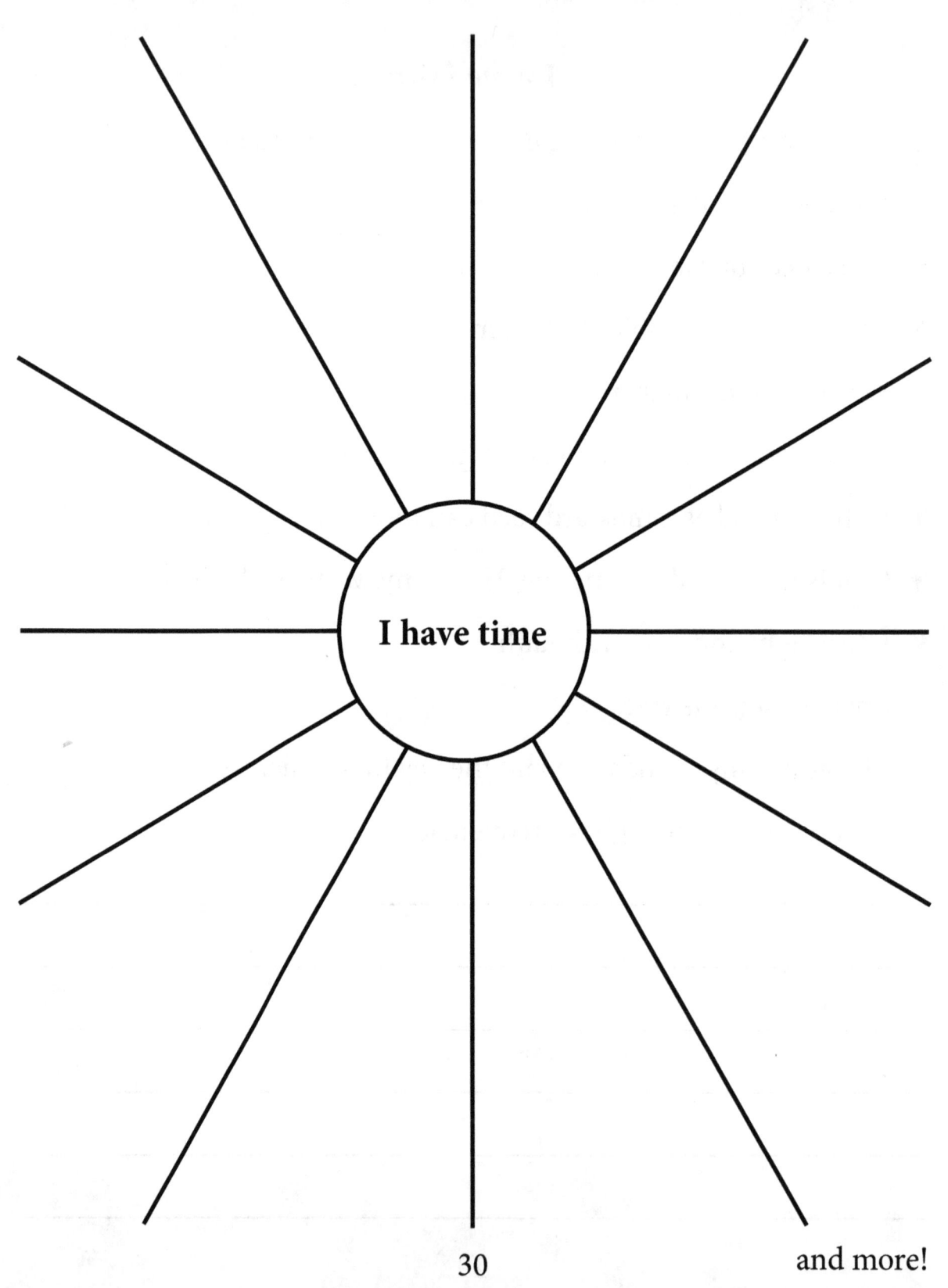

I have time

Variations: I always have enough time. I have enough time to/for …

- ♥ God promises length of days
- ♥ Time serves me well
- ♥ I have more than enough time every day
- ♥ With God I accomplish more every day and even more every year
- ♥ The time is now
- ♥ Today is a new day
- ♥ The past is done, in with the new
- ♥ Every moment is a perfect moment
- ♥ I always have plenty of time to finish what I desire
- ♥ Time is on my side
- ♥ Time helps me to stay focused
- ♥ There is always more time

_____

_____

_____

_____

_____

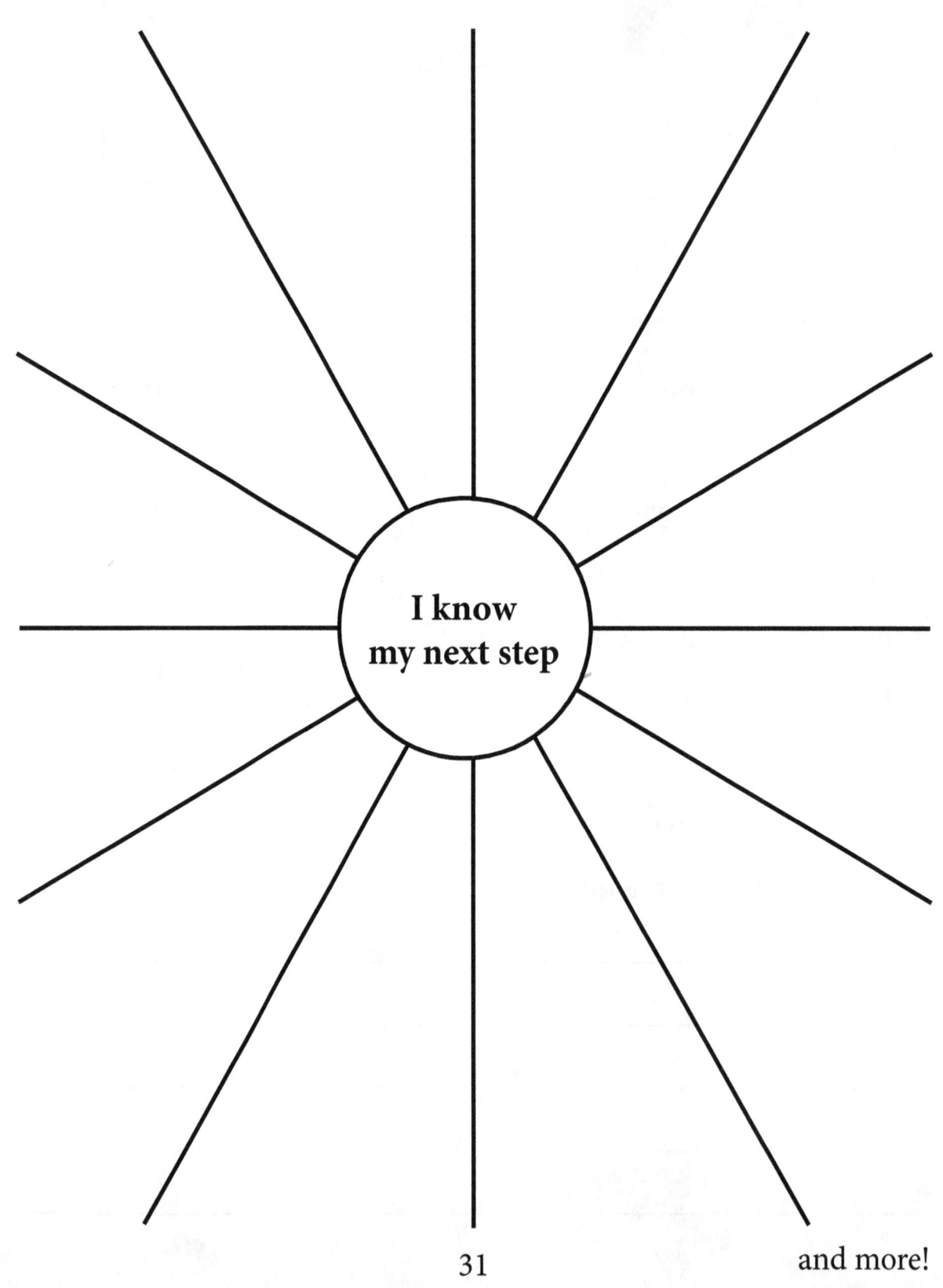

I know my next step

- ♥ I am focused on the solution
- ♥ All answers are already here
- ♥ I listen to God's guidance
- ♥ I rely on my gut feeling
- ♥ My path is laid out for me
- ♥ The best things are yet to come
- ♥ There is always a next and more
- ♥ Every step is part of my journey
- ♥ Opportunities are everywhere
- ♥ Doors and windows are open for me
- ♥ I plan my day
- ♥ I set goals and expect greatness

_____

_____

_____

_____

_____

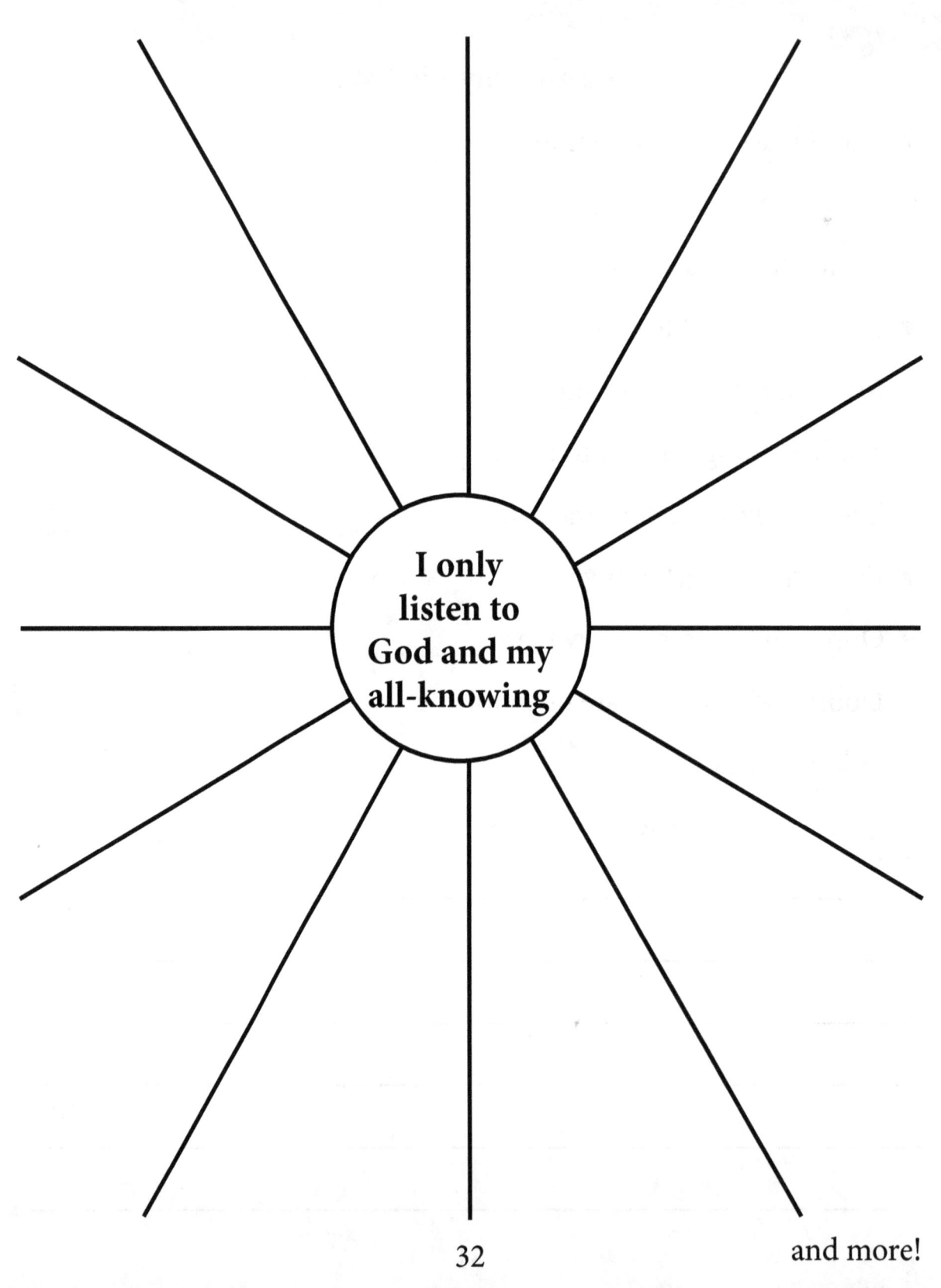

and more!

I only listen to God and my all-knowing

- ♥ I believe that God gave me an inner guidance system
- ♥ I stay focused
- ♥ There is only God and me
- ♥ My gut feelings guide me
- ♥ The answers are already here
- ♥ I know what is right
- ♥ God left me the Holy Bible containing instructions for a happy life
- ♥ I go forth in confidence
- ♥ I alone come before God in victory
- ♥ I practice the fruit of the Spirit
- ♥ I listen to my inspirations, leads, and nudges
- ♥ God is the ultimate truth

_____

_____

_____

_____

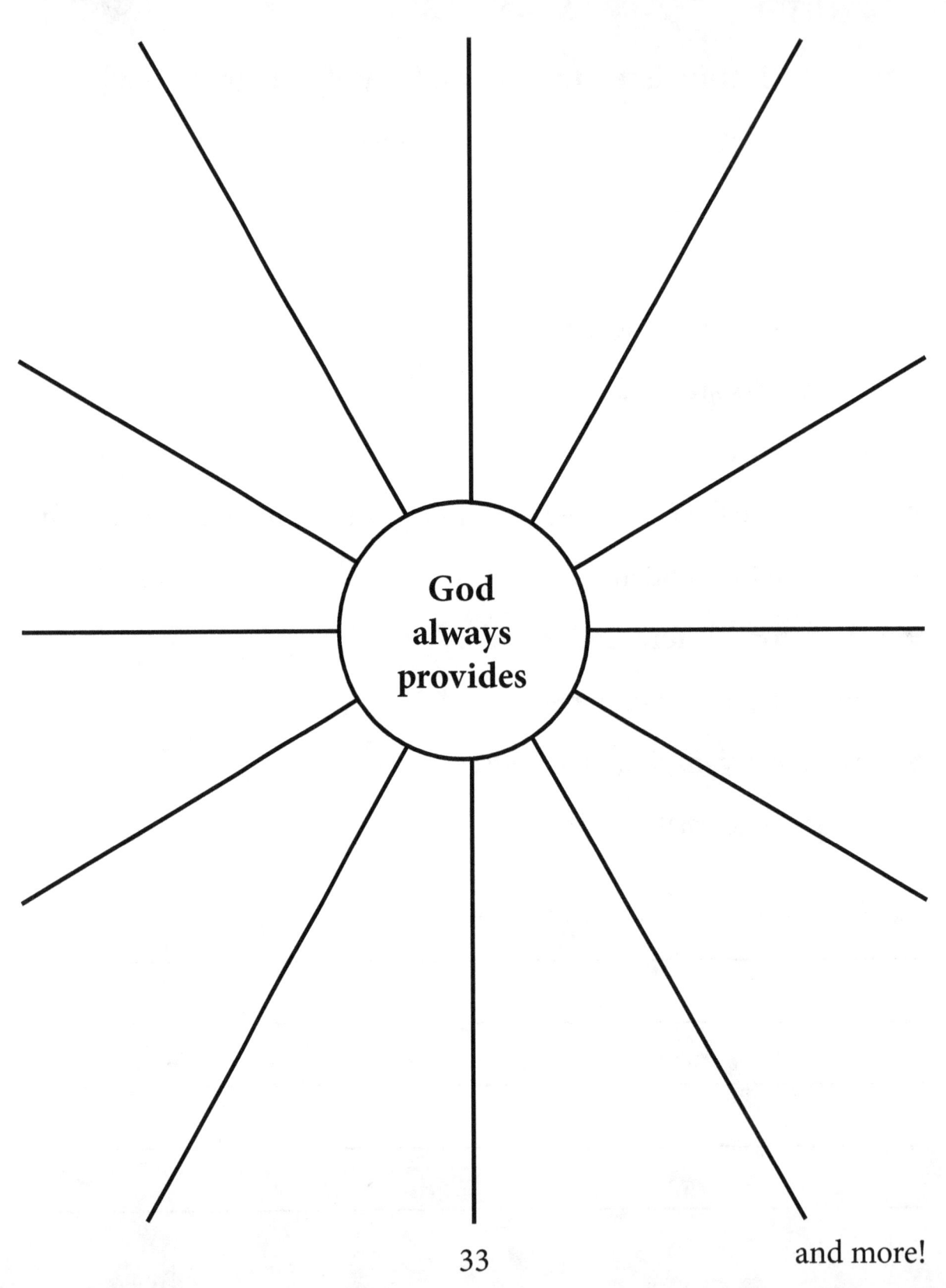

and more!

God always provides

- ♥ He provides for the sparrows and so much more for me
- ♥ He has provided for me in the past and will continue to provide
- ♥ I believe in God's promises
- ♥ My life is full of abundance
- ♥ I have a lot of stuff
- ♥ Life gets better and better
- ♥ There is variety and abundance everywhere
- ♥ God takes care of me
- ♥ I trust in Him
- ♥ The Universe is continually expanding
- ♥ God is with us forever
- ♥ God owns everything

_____

_____

_____

_____

_____

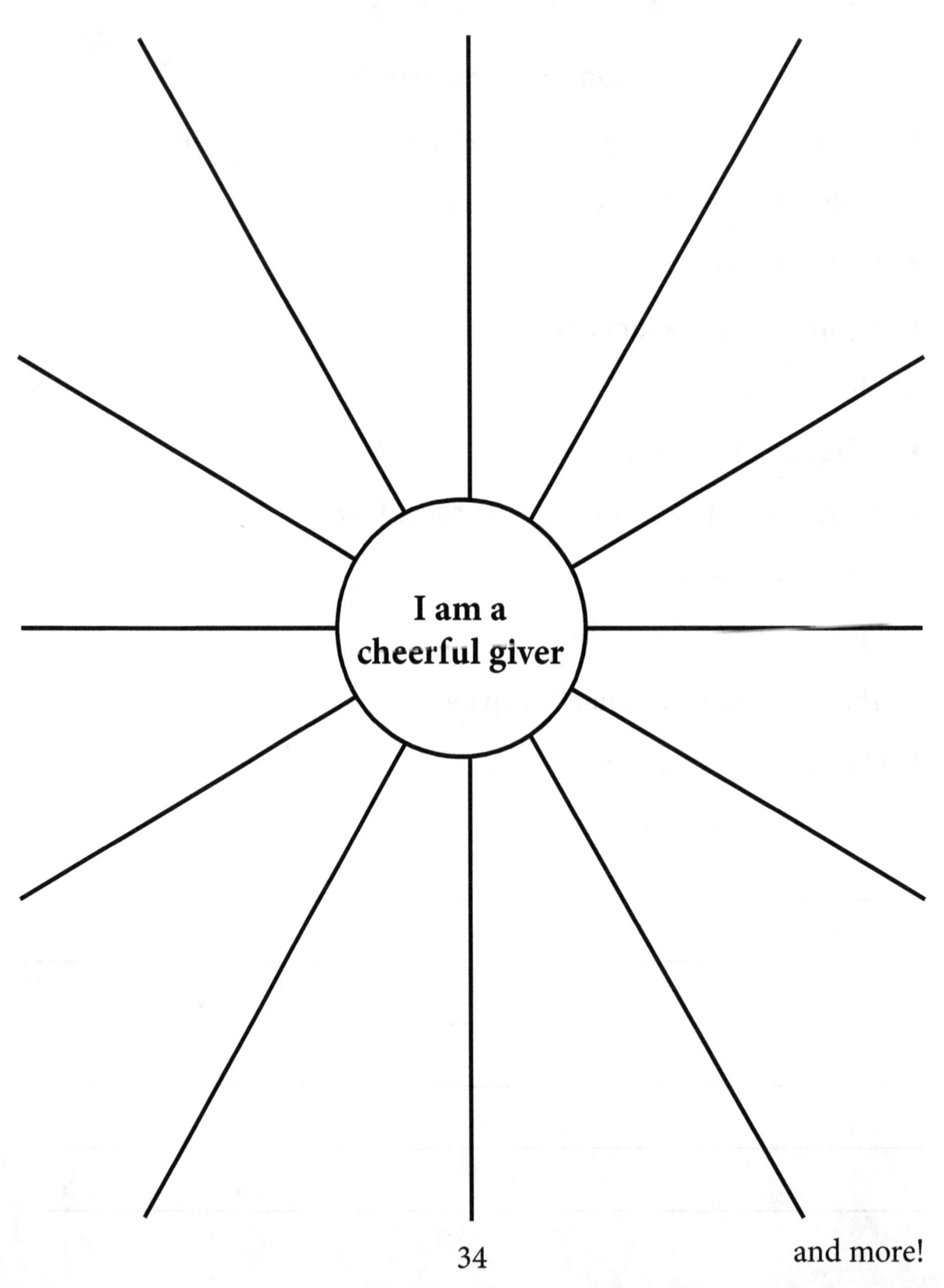

I am a cheerful giver

- ♥ I enjoy giving
- ♥ Giving and receiving are a balanced cycle
- ♥ I reap what I sow
- ♥ Contribution is a basic requirement for humans
- ♥ God loves for me to be a cheerful giver
- ♥ I have time, money, and talents to give
- ♥ The more I give the more I receive
- ♥ Everything I give comes back to me multiplied
- ♥ Giving makes me feel good
- ♥ I have a giving personality
- ♥ Jesus came to serve, He is the gift and the giver
- ♥ God commands me to love my neighbor as I love myself

_____

_____

_____

_____

_____

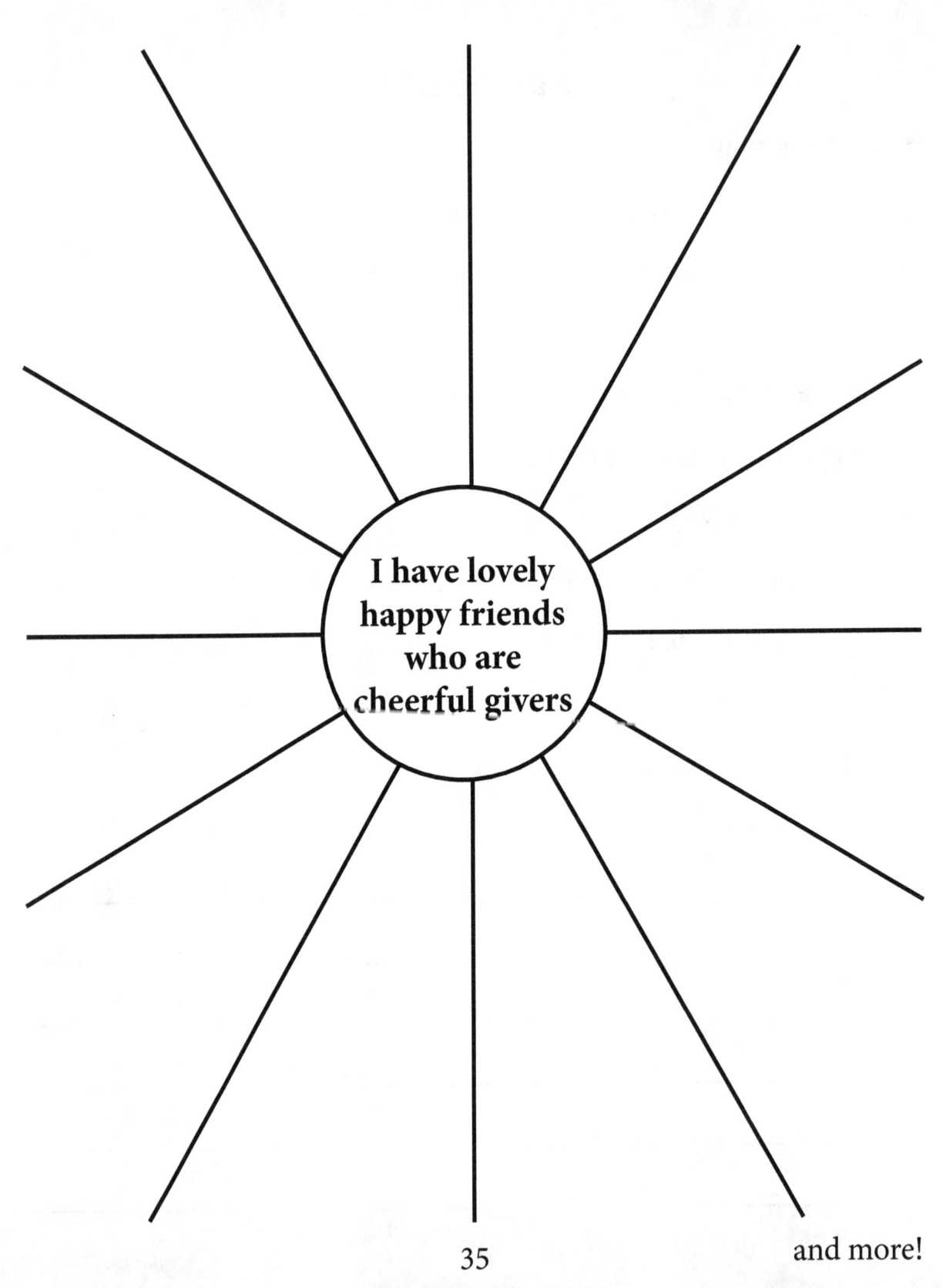

and more!

I have lovely happy friends who are cheerful givers

- ♥ I share moments with people who are nice to me
- ♥ I enjoy the company of happy, cheerful people
- ♥ I accept the encouragement of positive happy people
- ♥ I enjoy sharing
- ♥ I am my best friend
- ♥ I speak kind words to everyone and receive them in return
- ♥ I voice my love and appreciation for myself and friends
- ♥ I accept my friends as they are
- ♥ I am a happy lovely friend myself and I attract likeminded people
- ♥ I remember my friend's birthdays and they celebrate mine with me
- ♥ I choose happy, fun friends
- ♥ I like to participate in fun activities with my friends

_____

_____

_____

_____

_____

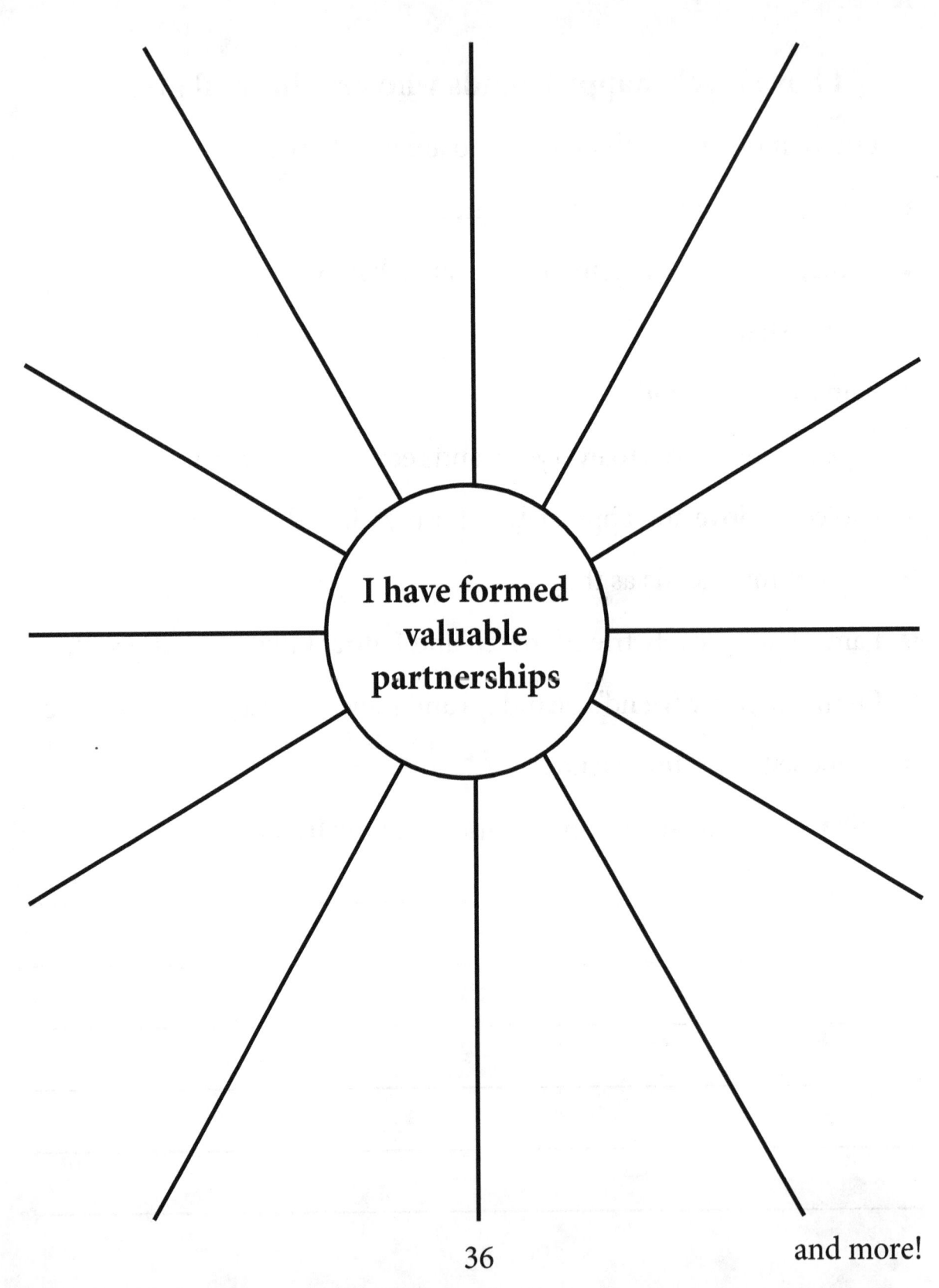

and more!

I have formed valuable partnerships

- ♥ I form partnerships easily
- ♥ I understand the value of partnering with friends and colleagues
- ♥ I have a best friend
- ♥ I have a prayer partner
- ♥ I have an accountability partner
- ♥ I have a business partner
- ♥ The Universe is set up to answer the prayers of two or more agreeing energies
- ♥ Partnerships encourage and support me
- ♥ Partnerships are empowering
- ♥ I share my askings and goals with my prayer partner
- ♥ I have a group to manifest and have fun with
- ♥ I ask my partners for help

_____

_____

_____

_____

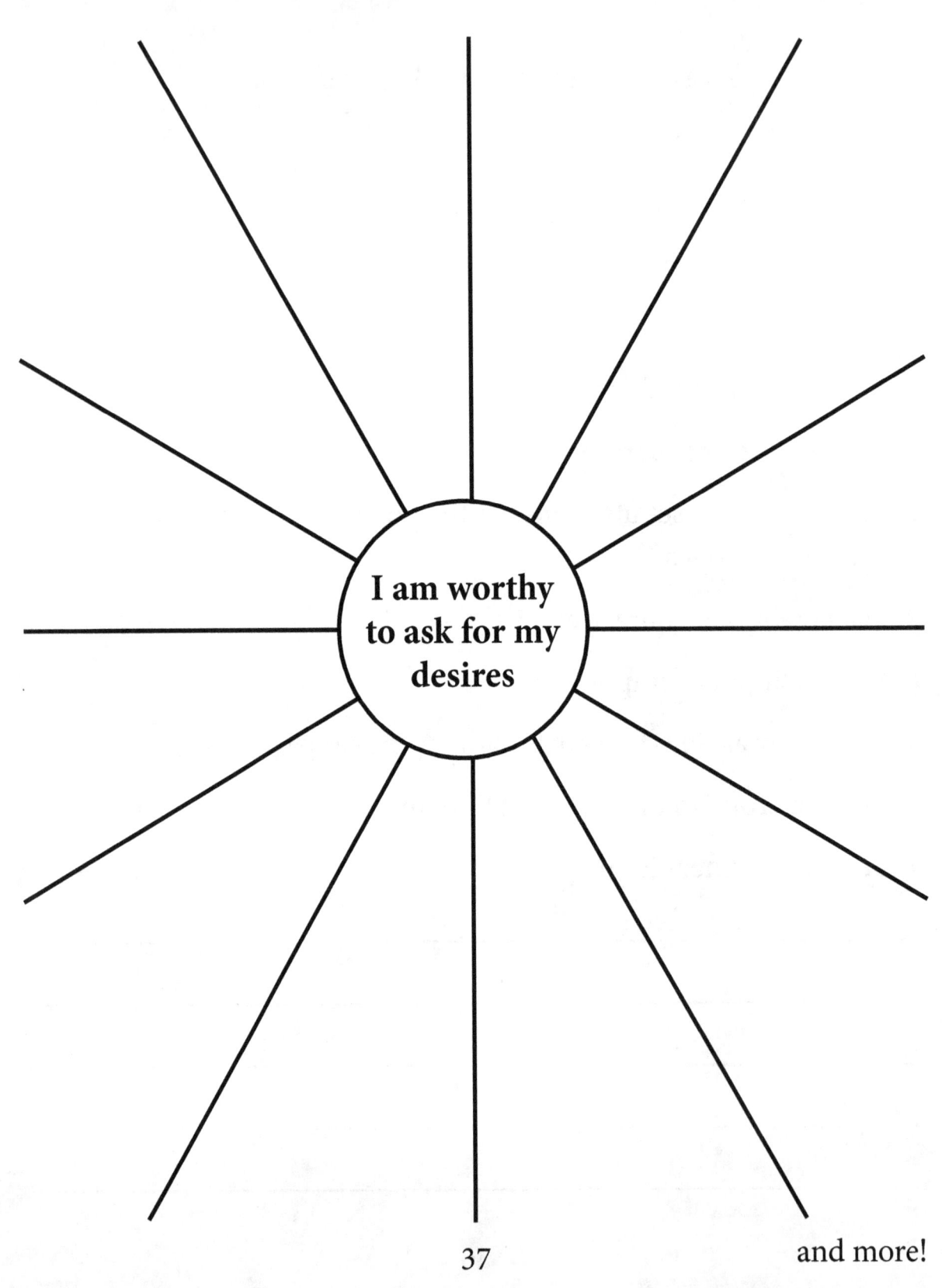

and more!

I am worthy to ask for my desires

♥ I am made in God's image and likeness

♥ I ask and I receive

♥ God desires for me to ask, petition, and make my heart known

♥ The Bible tells me so

♥ God's arms are around me, His love is in my heart

♥ God and I have great plans for me

♥ He blesses me and multiplies everything in my life

♥ God wishes to hear from me

♥ God loves me, I love God, I love myself

♥ I believe in myself

♥ I do good works

♥ I build my asking muscle

_____

_____

_____

_____

_____

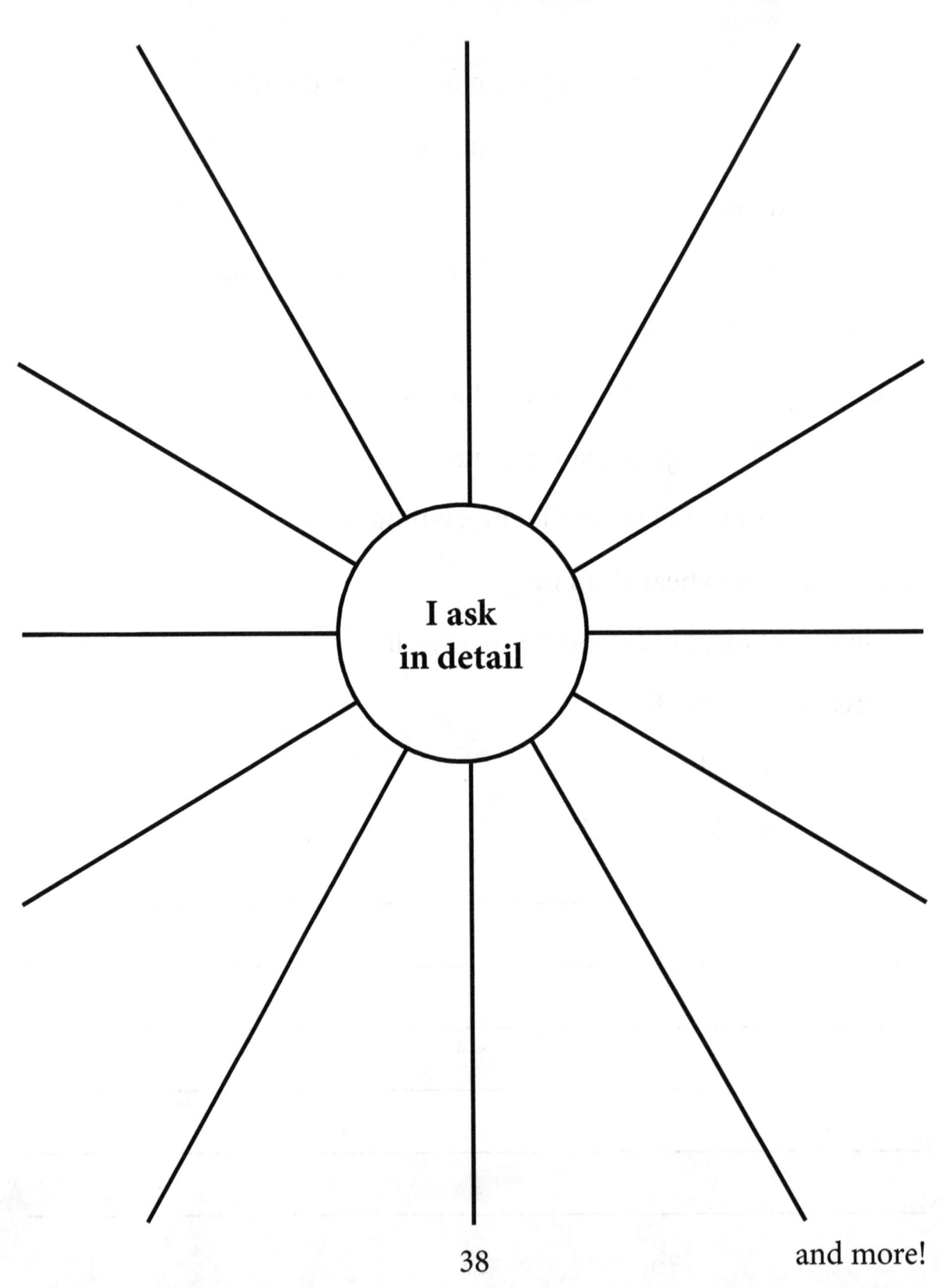

I ask in detail

- ♥ God and His Universe are very precise
- ♥ Details make my heart known even more
- ♥ The fun is in the details
- ♥ Details show how huge my faith is
- ♥ The more I ask in detail the more I receive precisely what I require
- ♥ I include parameters around my askings
- ♥ I define a compelling why
- ♥ I give thanks before I begin asking
- ♥ My clarity helps me to pick up my orders
- ♥ I choose to receive my exact askings
- ♥ When I ask in detail I know exactly that the delivery is mine
- ♥ I love asking and visualizing in detail

_____

_____

_____

_____

_____

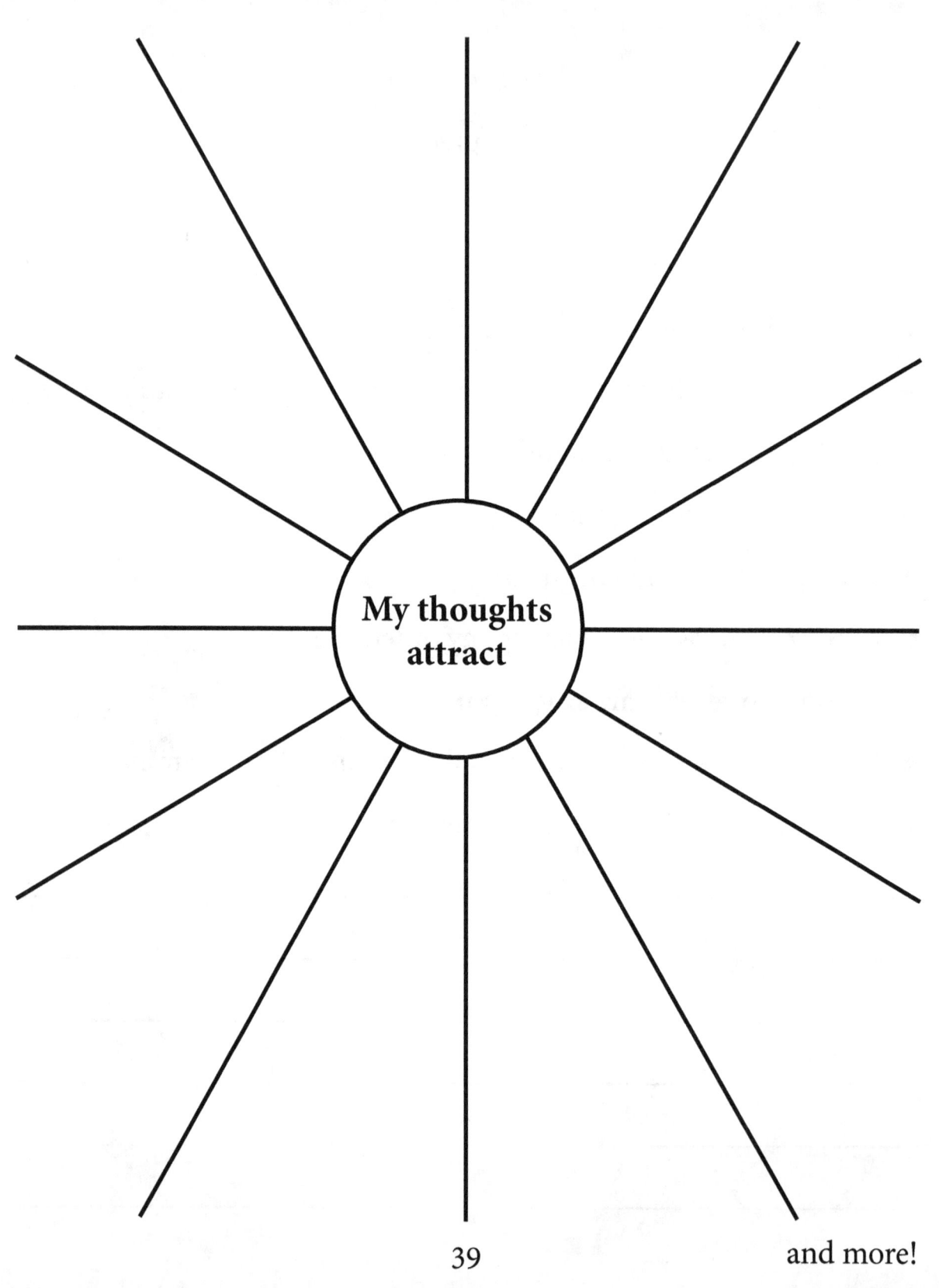

My thoughts attract

- ♥ I understand the Law of Attraction
- ♥ I monitor my thoughts
- ♥ Where focus goes energy flows
- ♥ I think many identical thoughts that match my desire
- ♥ I stay with my thoughts and ponder them for more than a minute
- ♥ Every vibration that radiates out of me comes back with a matching reaction
- ♥ My mind is a magnetic force
- ♥ Every answer is automatically summoned to me
- ♥ I am conscious of my thoughts
- ♥ I choose to think positive thoughts
- ♥ I think excellent and praiseworthy thoughts
- ♥ As a man thinks so is he

_____

_____

_____

_____

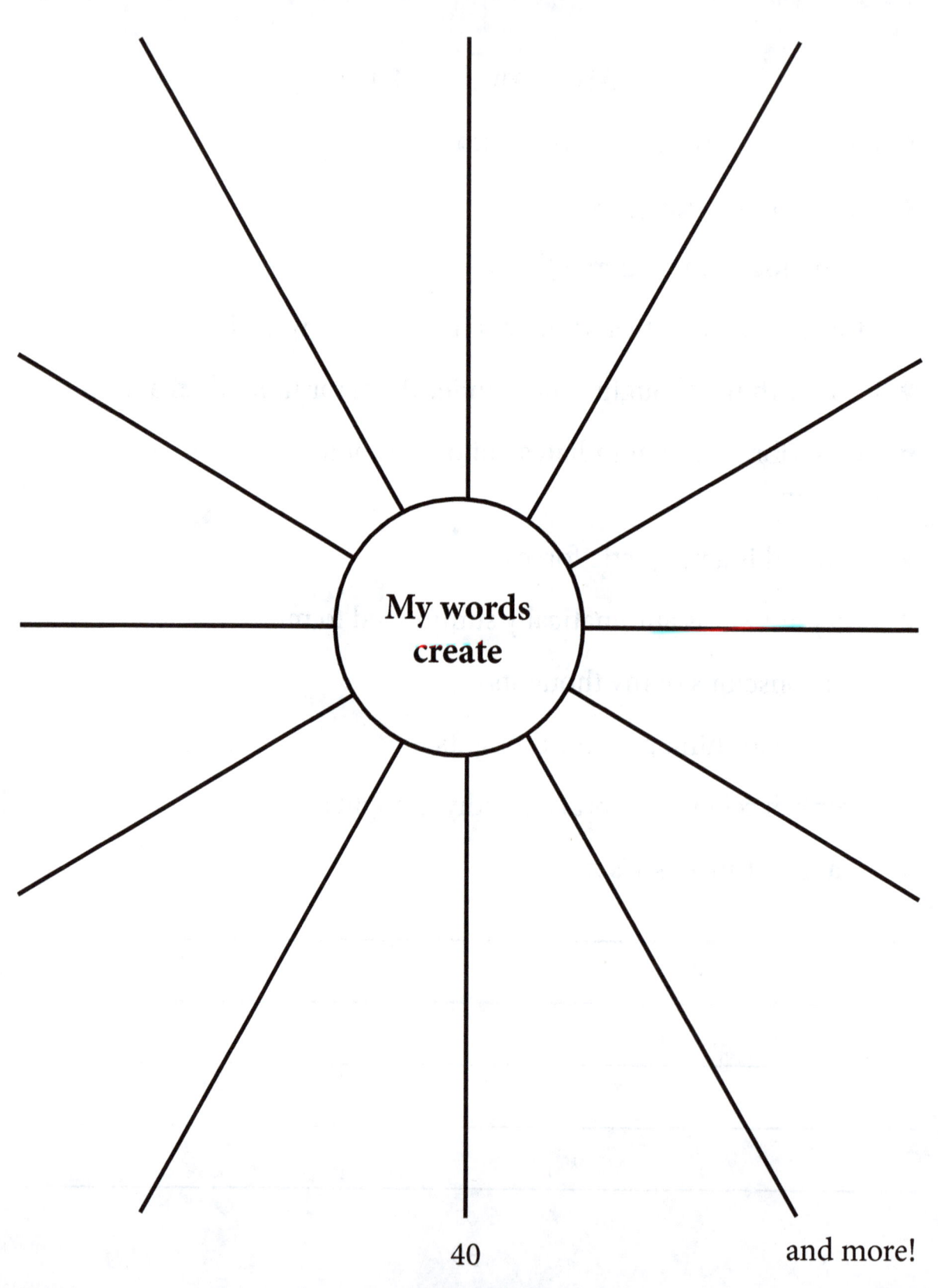

40 and more!

My words create

- ♥ My positive words create my positive life
- ♥ Every word that leaves my mouth comes back to me answered and fulfilled
- ♥ God spoke everything into existence
- ♥ The mouth speaks what the heart is full of
- ♥ Every word matters
- ♥ Words imprint water, we are over 70 percent water
- ♥ In the beginning was the Word
- ♥ The Word was with God and the Word was God
- ♥ I edit my words
- ♥ I speak over everything
- ♥ Jesus will return with the power of His tongue
- ♥ The word trumps the thought

_____

_____

_____

_____

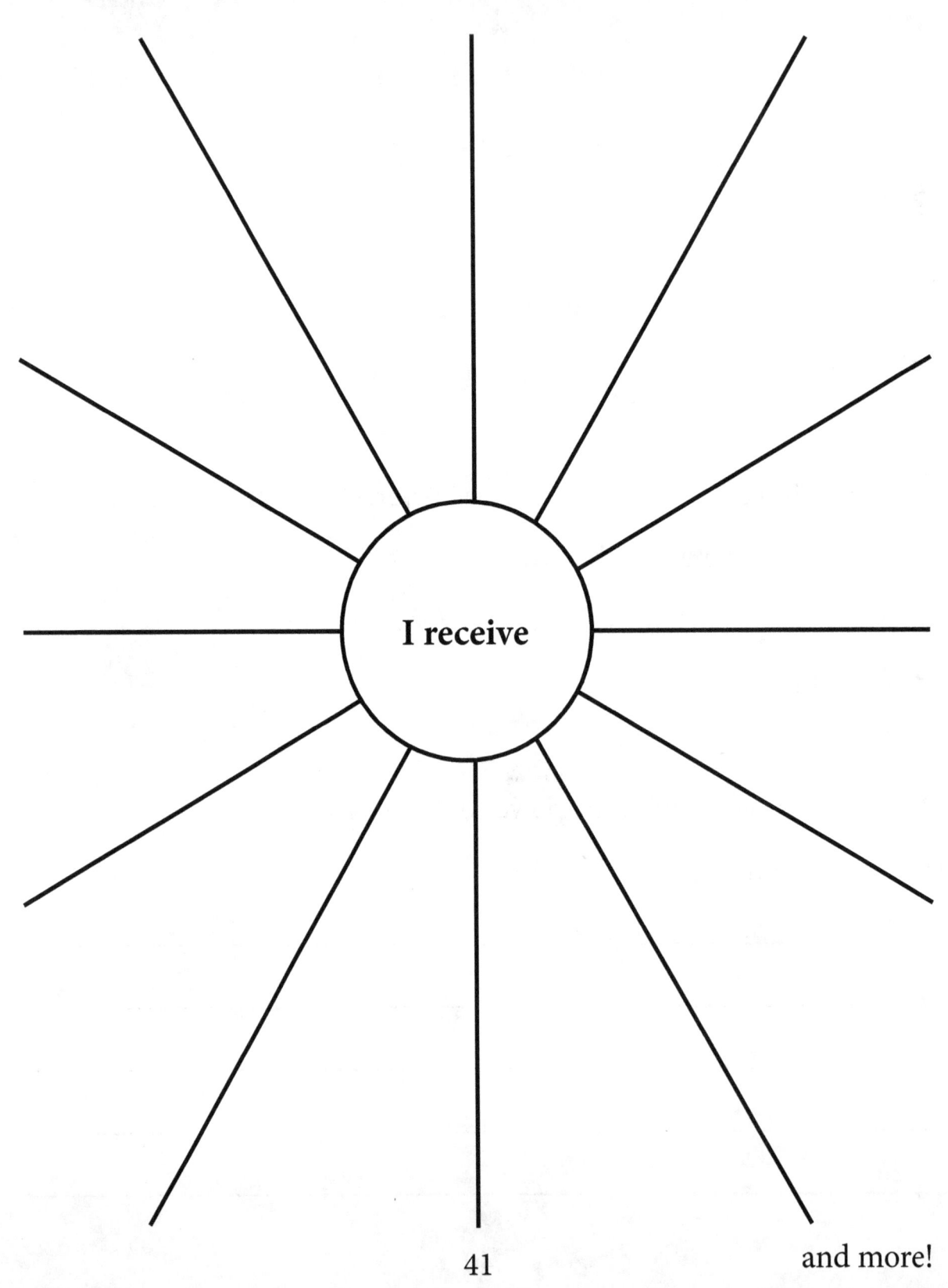

I receive

- ♥ My thoughts attract and my words create
- ♥ I reap what I sow
- ♥ My hands are wide open
- ♥ God has many gifts with my name on them, His divine storehouse is full of abundance that He intends to release to me
- ♥ I ask more so that I receive more
- ♥ I am the matching vibration
- ♥ I am ready to receive supernaturally
- ♥ I receive a continual flow of abundance
- ♥ I love to receive
- ♥ Everything I cheerfully give, returns to me multiplied
- ♥ I have faith to receive
- ♥ Ask and you shall receive

_____

_____

_____

_____

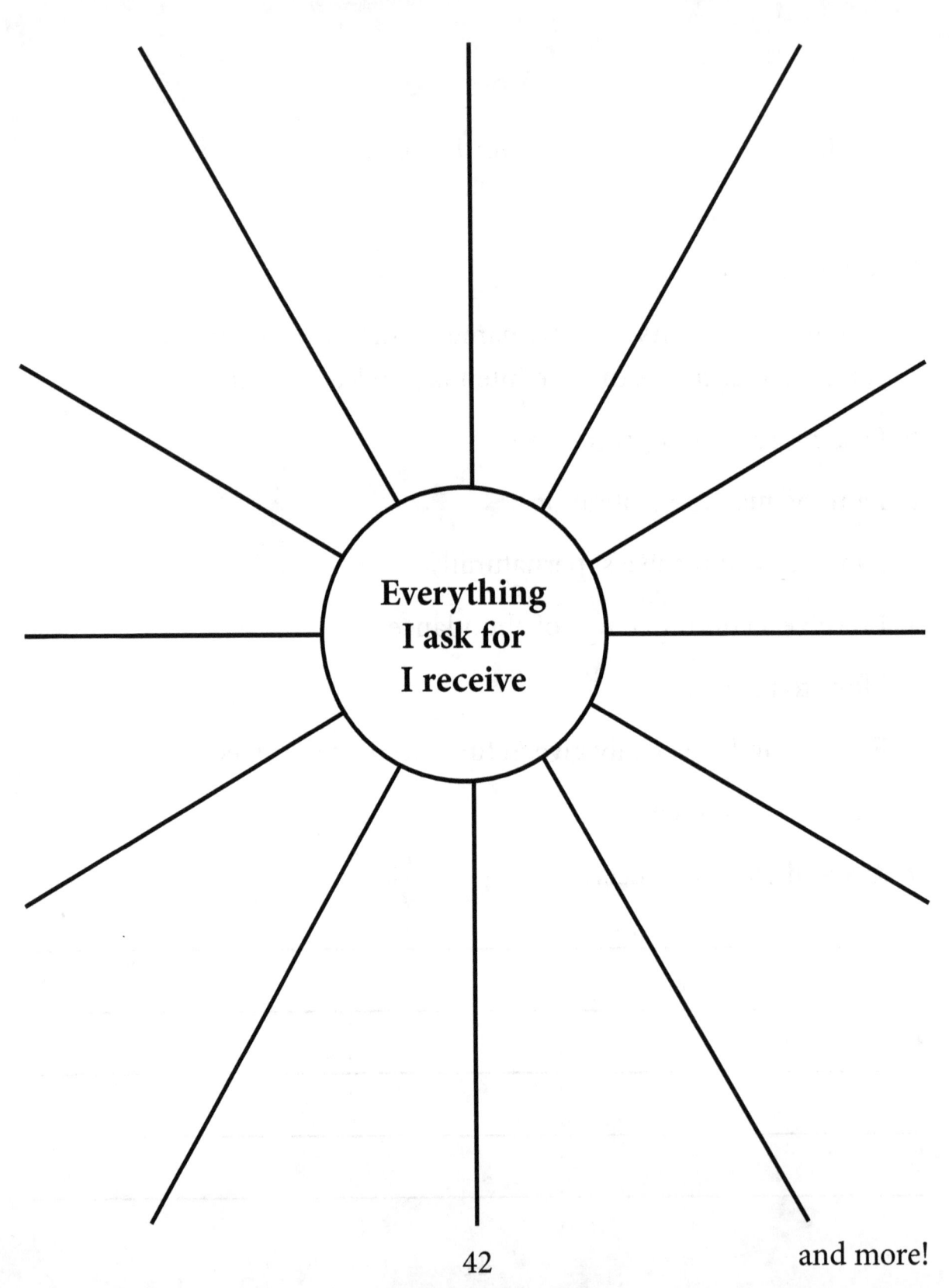

and more!

Everything I ask for I receive

- ♥ God set up this Universe as a divine delivery system
- ♥ Everyone who asks receives (Matt. 7:7-8)
- ♥ It is a spiritual absolute
- ♥ I am the matching vibration
- ♥ I am ready to receive
- ♥ God promises me in Matthew 7:7-8, Mark 11:24, John 16:24 and many other Bible verses that when I ask I shall receive
- ♥ I am a professional asker
- ♥ I understand the power of asking
- ♥ I have faith that it is already done
- ♥ I am able to speak and write
- ♥ My thoughts attract and my words create
- ♥ My words always return accomplished (Isaiah 55:11)

_____

_____

_____

_____

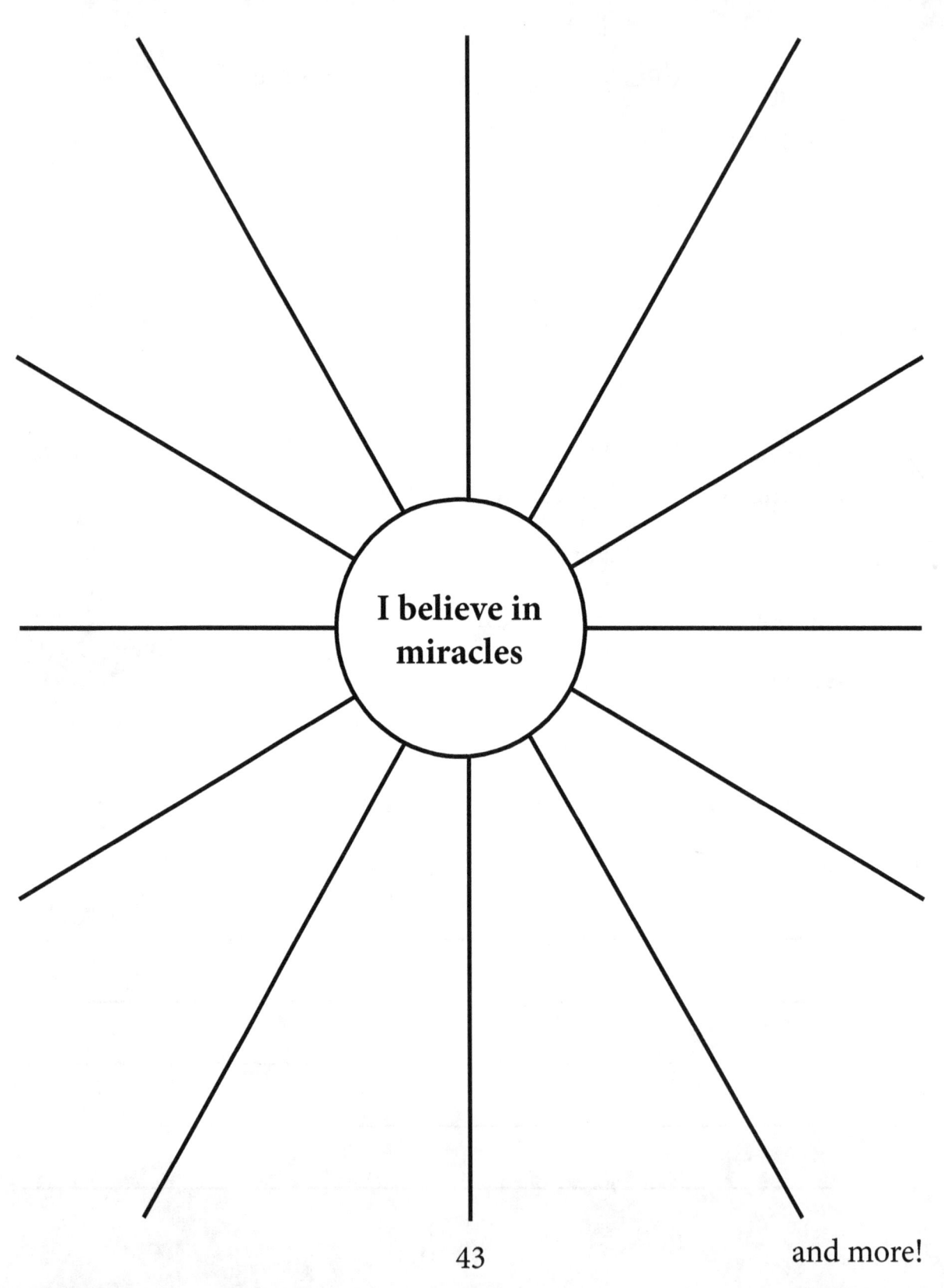
and more!

I believe in miracles

- ♥ Miracles happen all the time
- ♥ I have seen plenty of miracles in my life
- ♥ God is in the miracle business
- ♥ God is the same yesterday, today and tomorrow
- ♥ God is a miracle maker
- ♥ Miracles are everywhere
- ♥ I recognize the miracles around me
- ♥ I enjoy being wowed by God's miracles
- ♥ I keep track of the miracles in my life
- ♥ I receive miracles daily
- ♥ I ask for miracles every day
- ♥ God is supernatural

_____
_____
_____
_____
_____

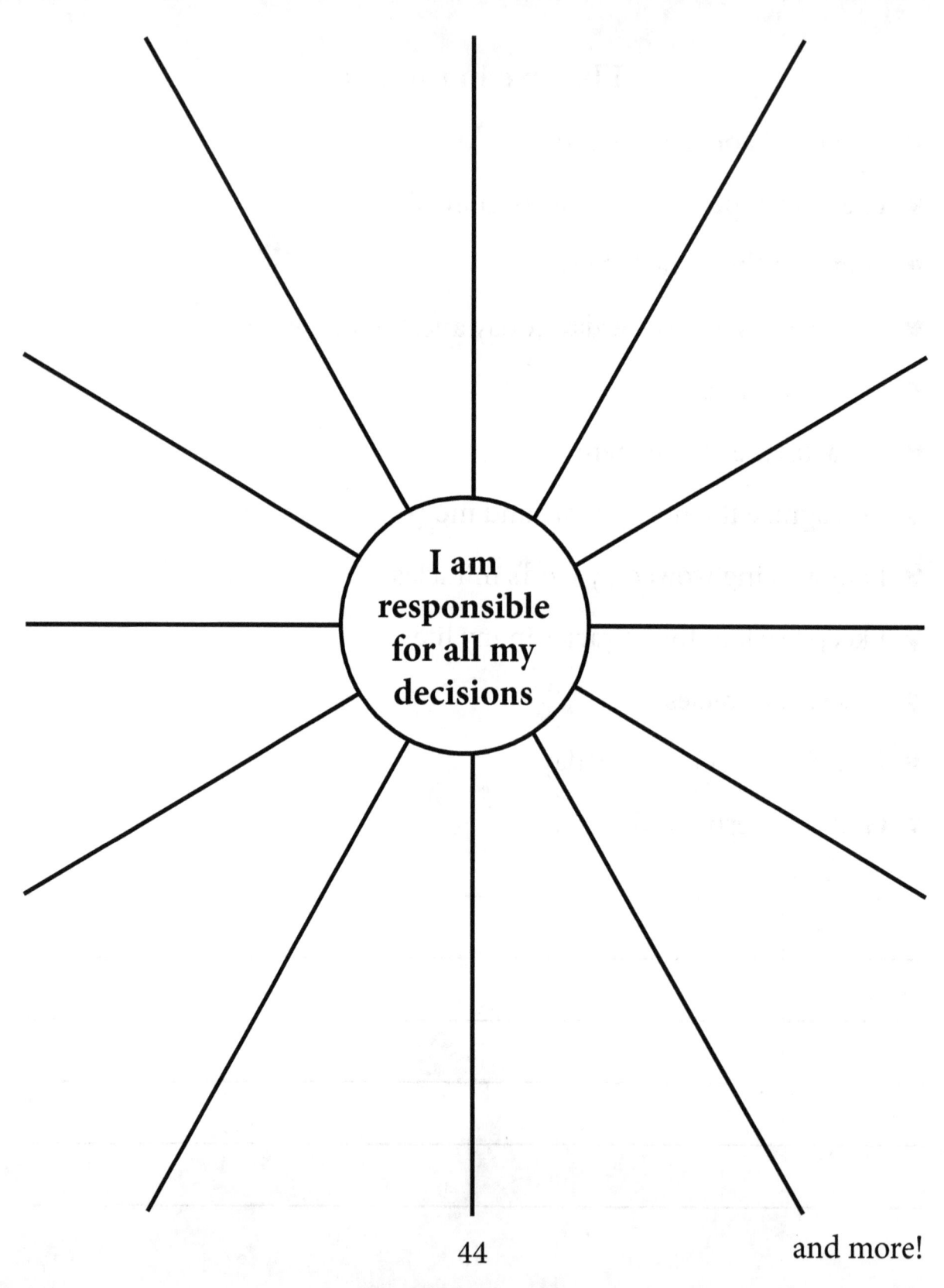

and more!

I am responsible for all my decisions

- ♥ I have signed every contract in my life
- ♥ I listen to my gut feelings and act on them
- ♥ It is all me
- ♥ There is only me and my Creator
- ♥ I pray before I make decisions
- ♥ My decisions brought me to where I am right now
- ♥ I welcome responsibility
- ♥ God is in control
- ♥ Making a decision feels powerful
- ♥ I trust in my ability to make the right decisions
- ♥ God guides my decision making
- ♥ My decision-making skills set me on the right path

_____

_____

_____

_____

_____

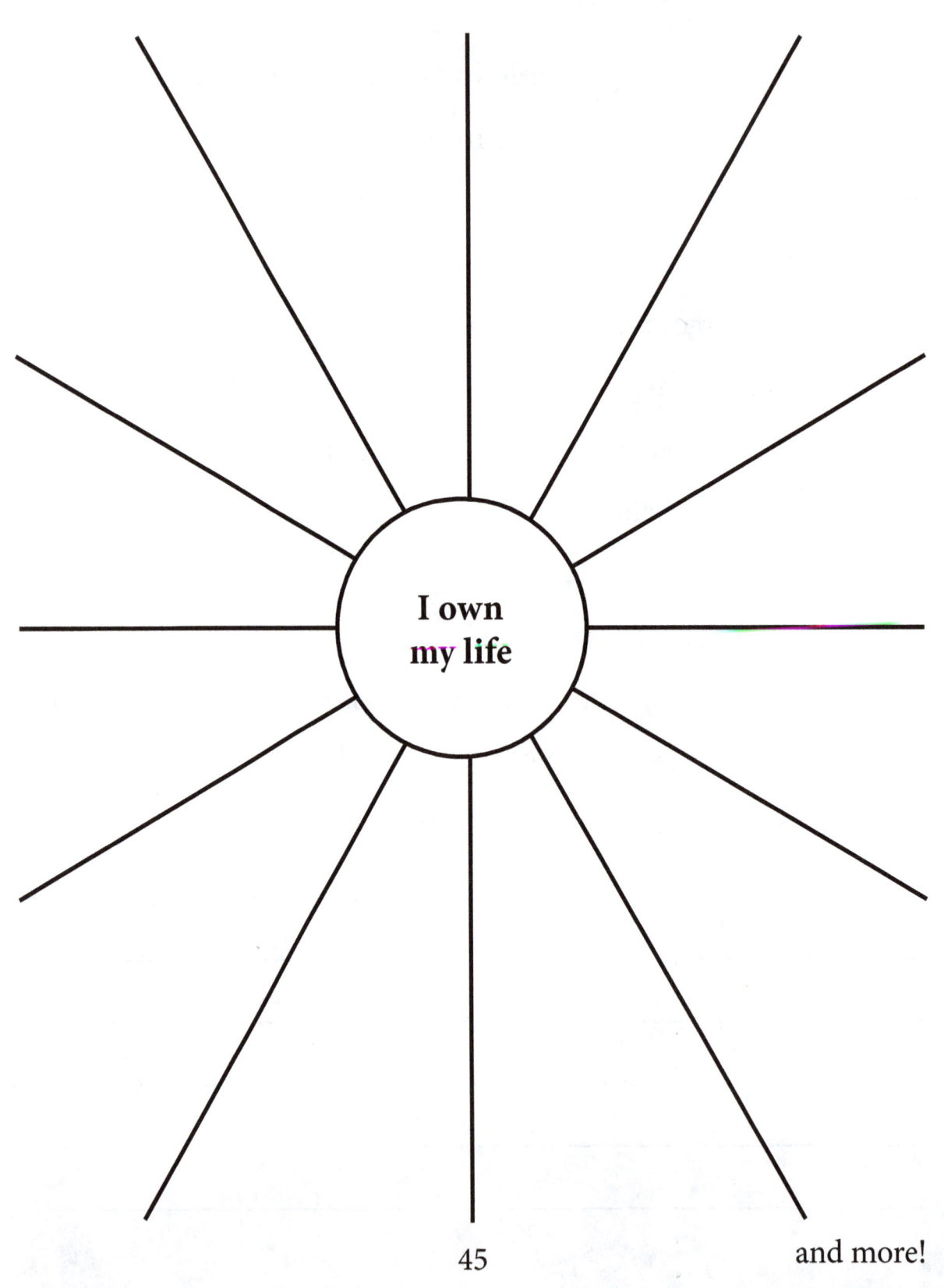

and more!

I own my life

Variations: I am responsible for my own life

- ♥ I made all my decisions, I signed all my contracts
- ♥ I understand that I am responsible for me
- ♥ I have the power to change everything in my life
- ♥ My positive attitude and positive words create my beautiful life
- ♥ I love my life
- ♥ I am happy and energized the moment my eyes open in the morning
- ♥ I am connected to my Creator
- ♥ I write my goals down
- ♥ I journal daily
- ♥ My life keeps growing
- ♥ I am better and better every day
- ♥ My life is centered around joy

_____

_____

_____

_____

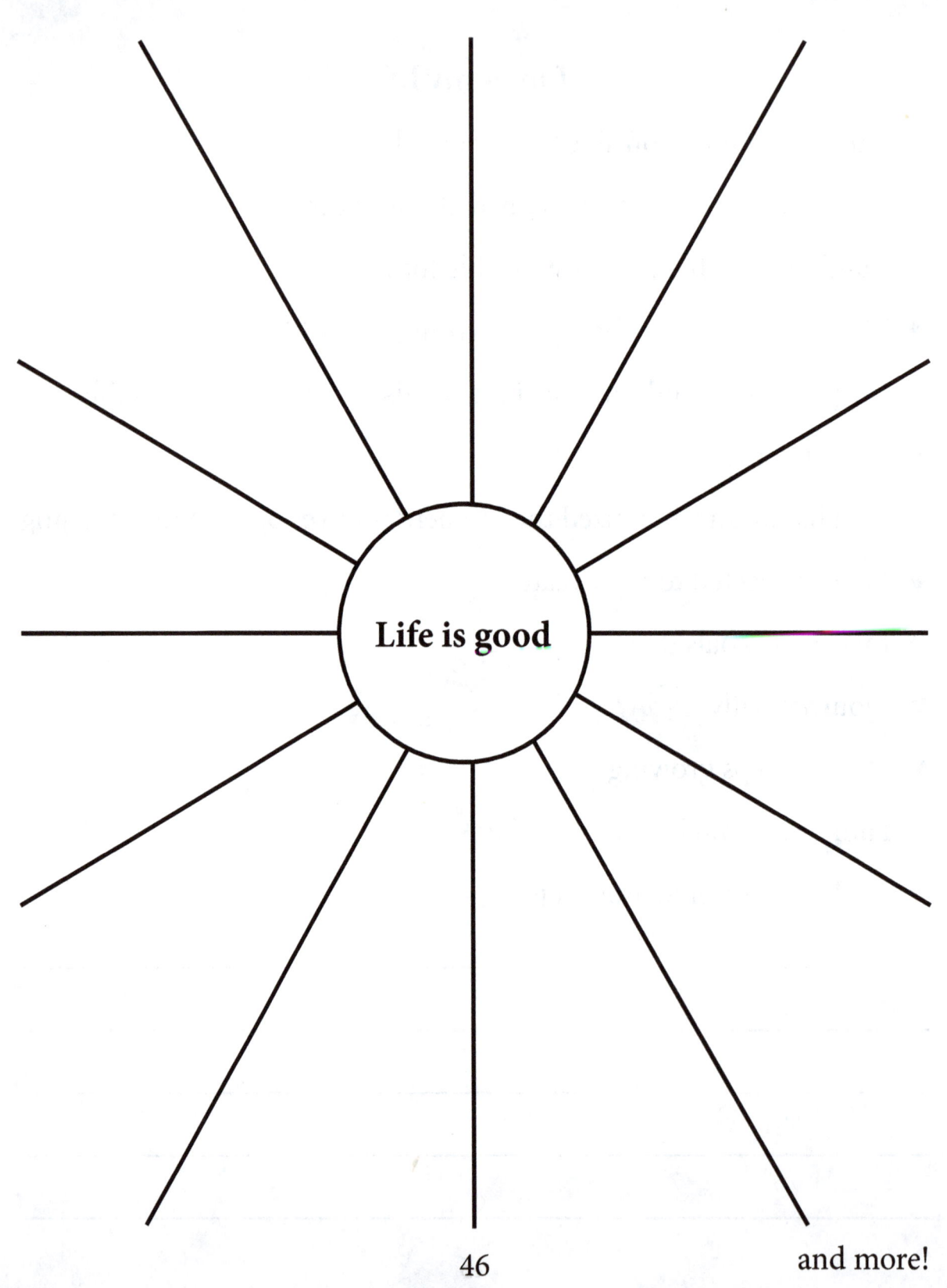

and more!

Life is good

- ♥ I enjoy myself daily
- ♥ I have fun, laugh, and smile
- ♥ I live in appreciation and gratitude
- ♥ I have everything I require, everything is provided for by God
- ♥ I have more than enough
- ♥ Life is light and easy
- ♥ I feel happy, healthy, and wealthy
- ♥ I see the abundance everywhere
- ♥ I have this life to enjoy
- ♥ God always provides for me
- ♥ I am alive and I thrive
- ♥ Goodness is the healthy option

_____

_____

_____

_____

_____

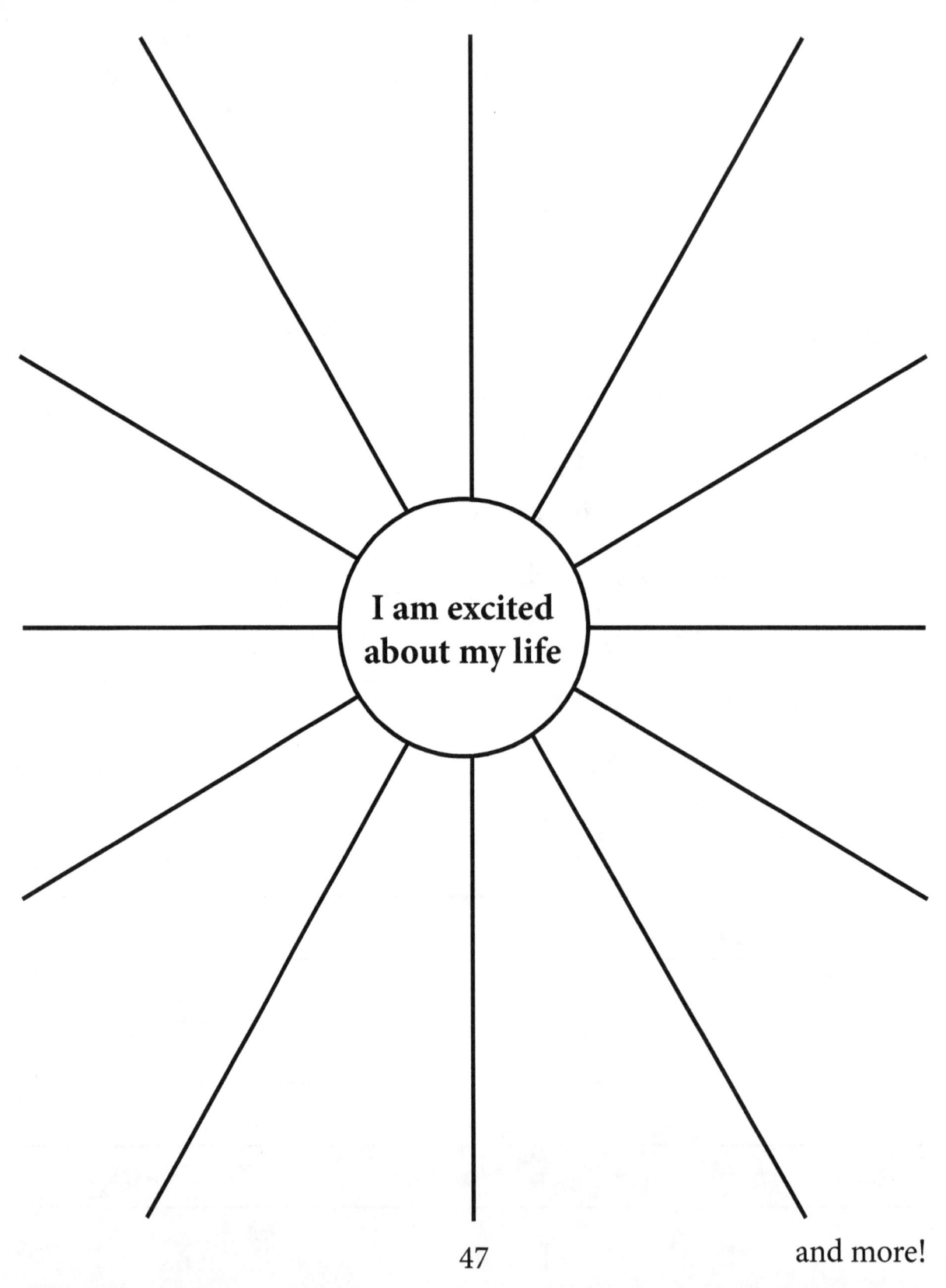

and more!

I am excited about my life

- ♥ I laugh often
- ♥ I light up the room when I walk in
- ♥ My life is better and better all the time
- ♥ Each day and every situation brings me joy
- ♥ I love my life
- ♥ I am so excited to play with my things
- ♥ I have wonderful friends that love me
- ♥ My life's work is my passion
- ♥ I am growing spiritually, mentally, physically, and financially all the time
- ♥ I have fun every day
- ♥ I continue to create the life of my dreams
- ♥ I have so much fun being me

_____

_____

_____

_____

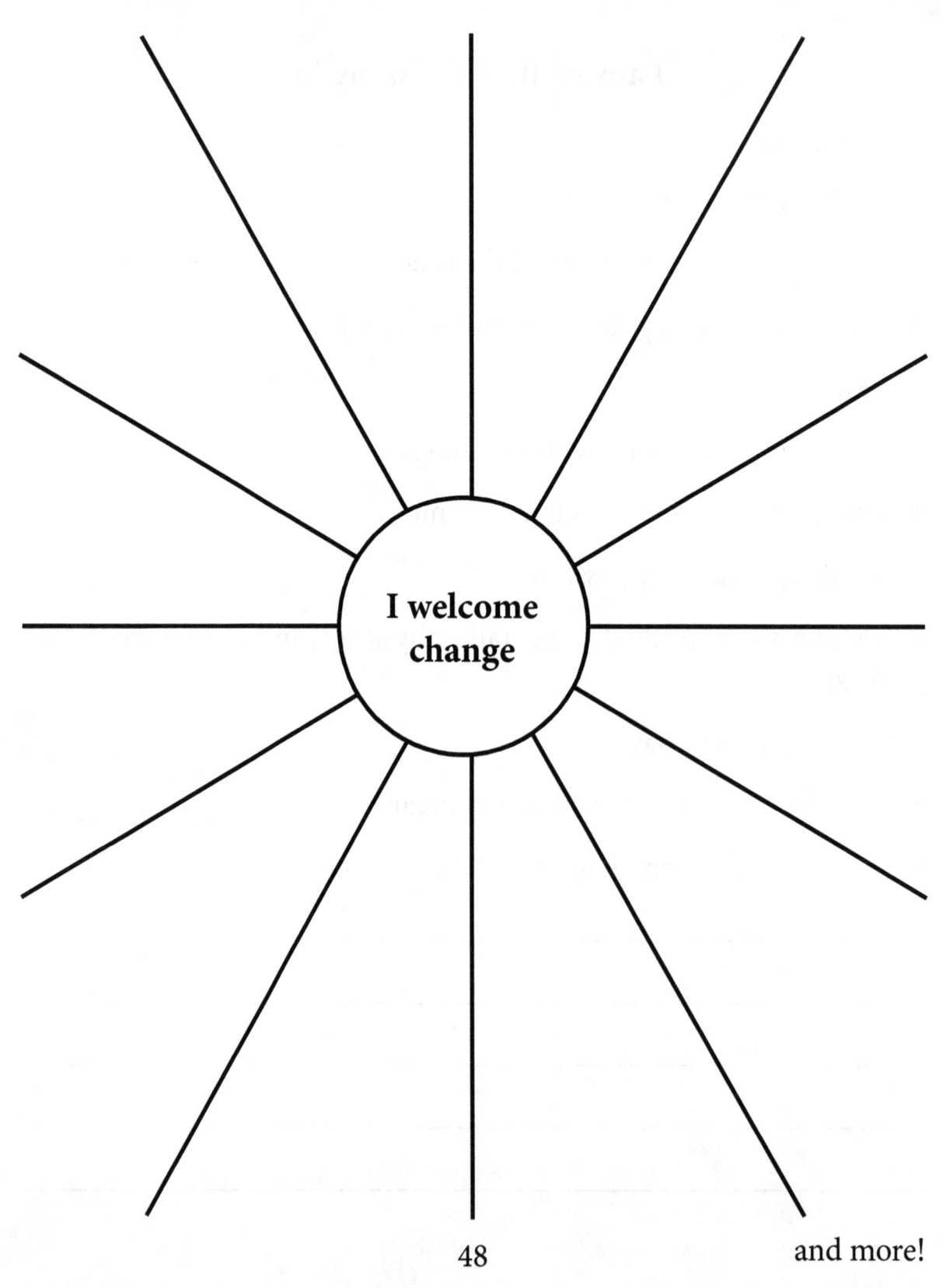

and more!

I welcome change

- ♥ I am new every day
- ♥ Change is healthy and good
- ♥ Change is exciting
- ♥ I can depend on change
- ♥ Change keeps life interesting
- ♥ Desire for change sparks growth
- ♥ Change is motivating
- ♥ Out with the old, in with the new
- ♥ Happy new day
- ♥ I have changed many times before and I turned out great
- ♥ Change brings with it the promise of a bright future
- ♥ We are born to grow, expand, and change

_____

_____

_____

_____

_____

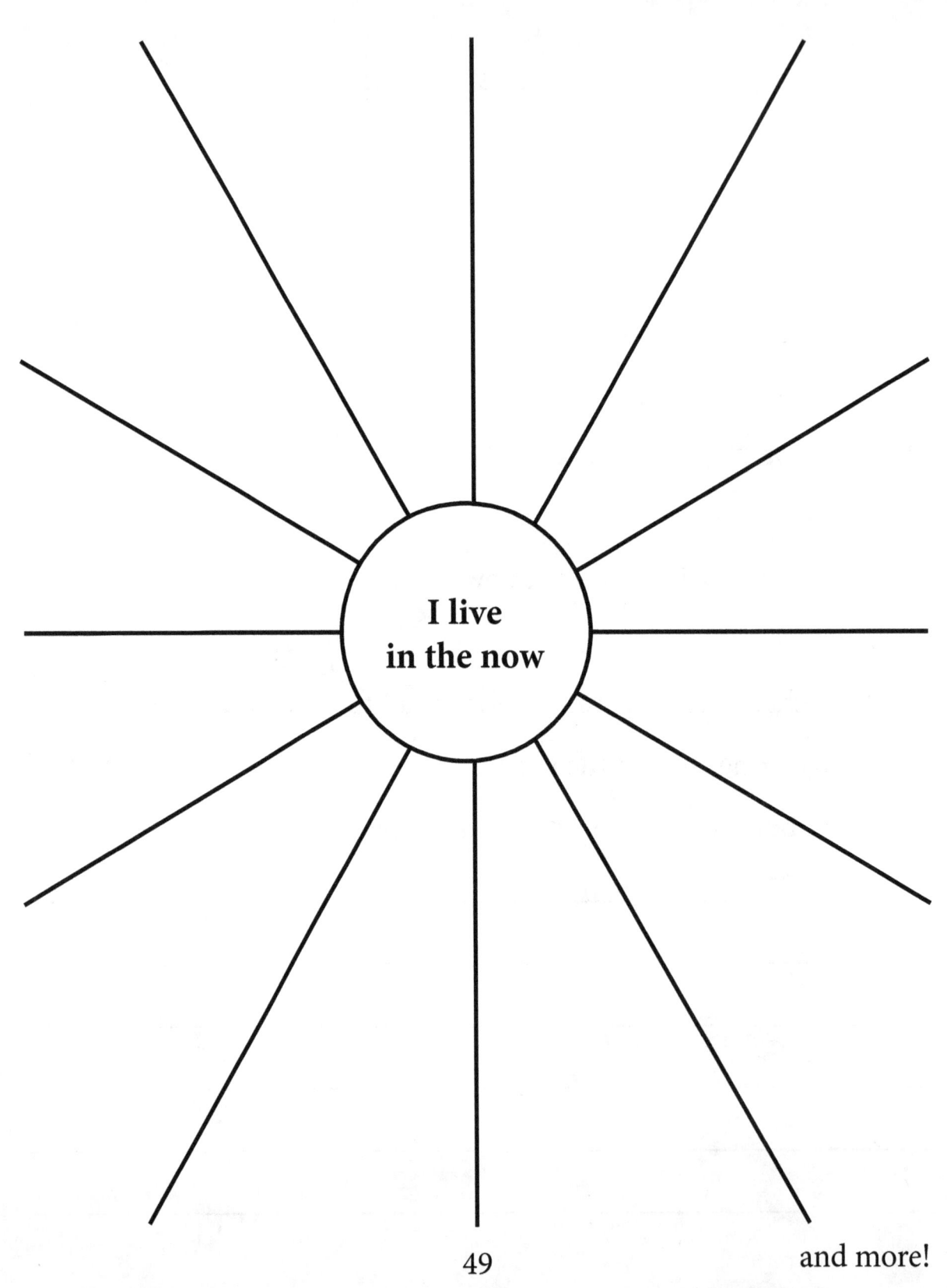

and more!

I live in the now

- ♥ Everything happens in the now
- ♥ Every day I am made new
- ♥ Everything is made new in Christ
- ♥ I am content with myself
- ♥ All change happens in the present moment
- ♥ I am aligned to my divine path
- ♥ I recognize myself as the co-creator of my life
- ♥ I find joy in the things I am doing today
- ♥ There is only here and now
- ♥ I choose to be in the present moment at all times
- ♥ I am focused
- ♥ God planned everything from the beginning to the end, thus I can rejoice in the present moment

_____
_____
_____
_____

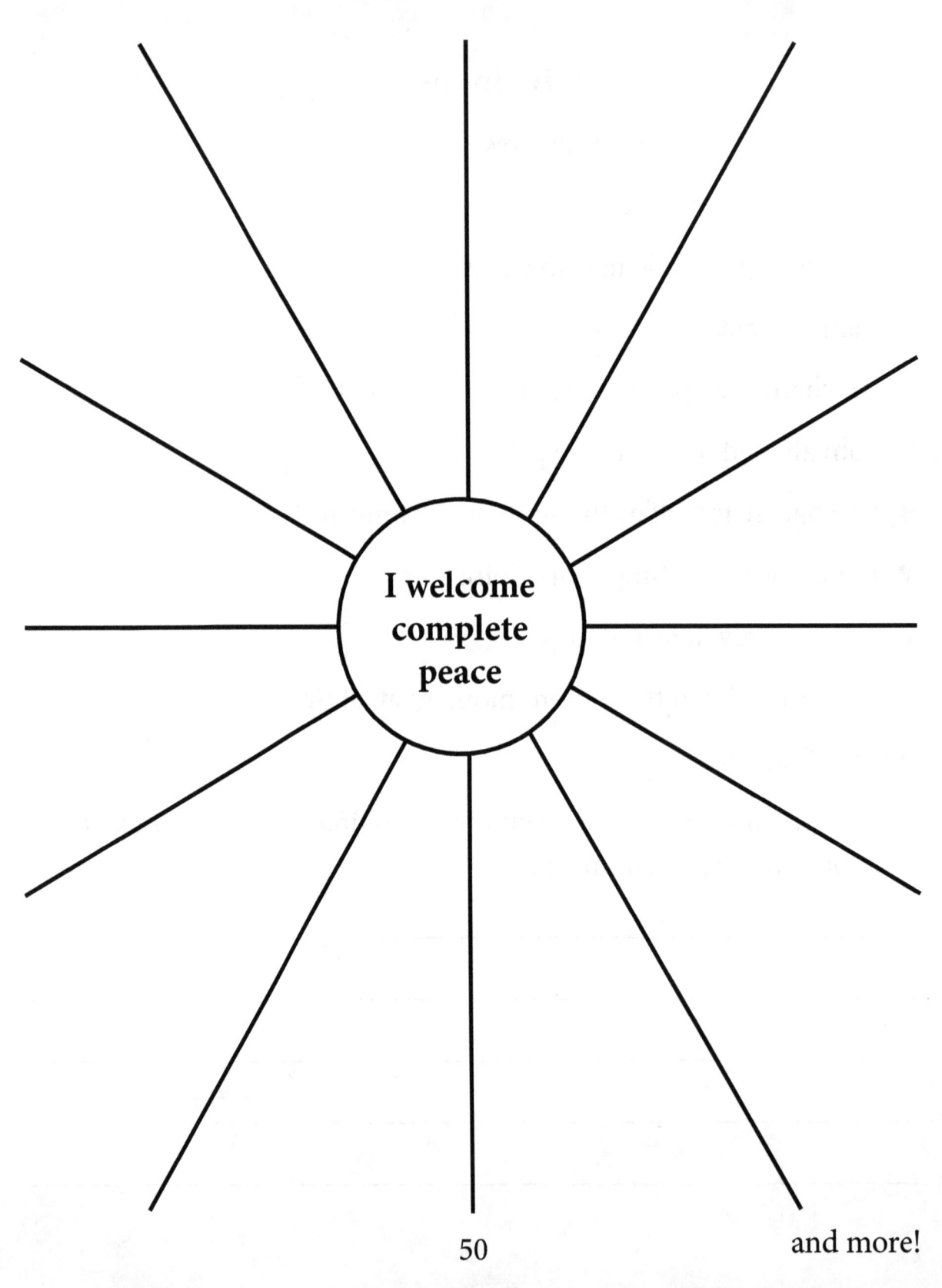

and more!

I welcome complete peace

Variations: I allow peace within me and in my environment.

- ♥ My life is harmonious
- ♥ God is always with me
- ♥ All things are possible all the time
- ♥ I meditate and sit quietly listening to God daily
- ♥ I follow my breath
- ♥ I am grateful for my breath of life
- ♥ All is well all the time
- ♥ I am happy
- ♥ I accept myself and others exactly as we are
- ♥ I am calm
- ♥ I am relaxed
- ♥ My head is aligned with my heart

_____

_____

_____

_____

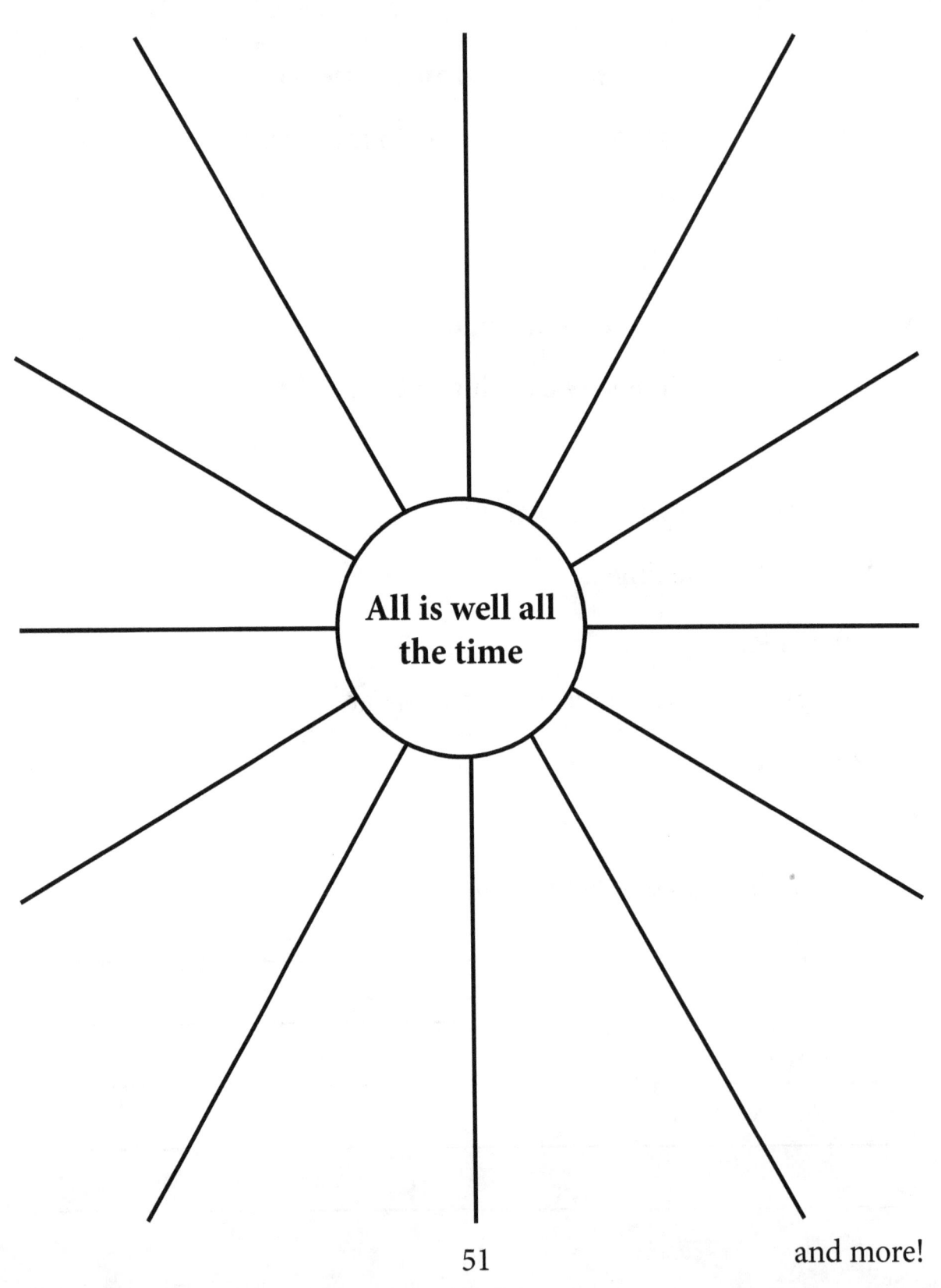

and more!

All is well all the time

- ♥ God planned everything, He is the beginning and the end
- ♥ I live in neutrality
- ♥ I see the good in all
- ♥ I am love. Love is the answer
- ♥ God is in control
- ♥ I accept everything as it is
- ♥ God blesses me
- ♥ Everything that is mine finds its way to me
- ♥ I enjoy sharing random acts of kindness
- ♥ I believe in myself and others
- ♥ God has done it all, He has done a complete work
- ♥ I do the right thing

_____

_____

_____

_____

_____

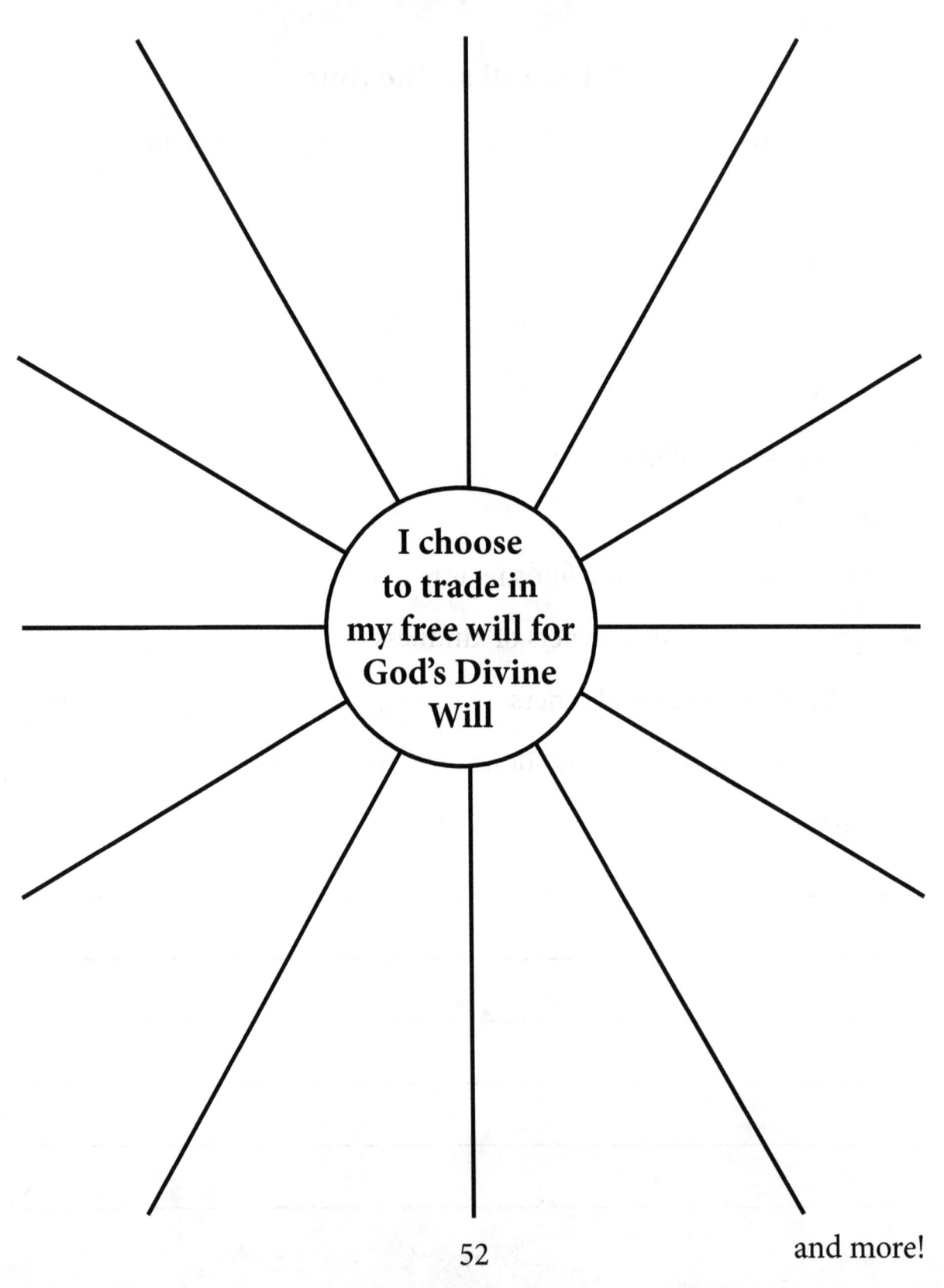

I choose to trade in my free will for God's Divine Will

- ♥ I live in the Tree of Life
- ♥ I focus on the good in everything
- ♥ Love is the answer to every question
- ♥ Love is everywhere
- ♥ I choose to be positive
- ♥ I choose to be yoked to Christ
- ♥ I view my world friendly
- ♥ I understand the power of Oneness
- ♥ I align my will with God's Divine Will
- ♥ On Earth as it is in Heaven
- ♥ I am one with God
- ♥ I am made in His image and likeness

_____

_____

_____

_____

_____

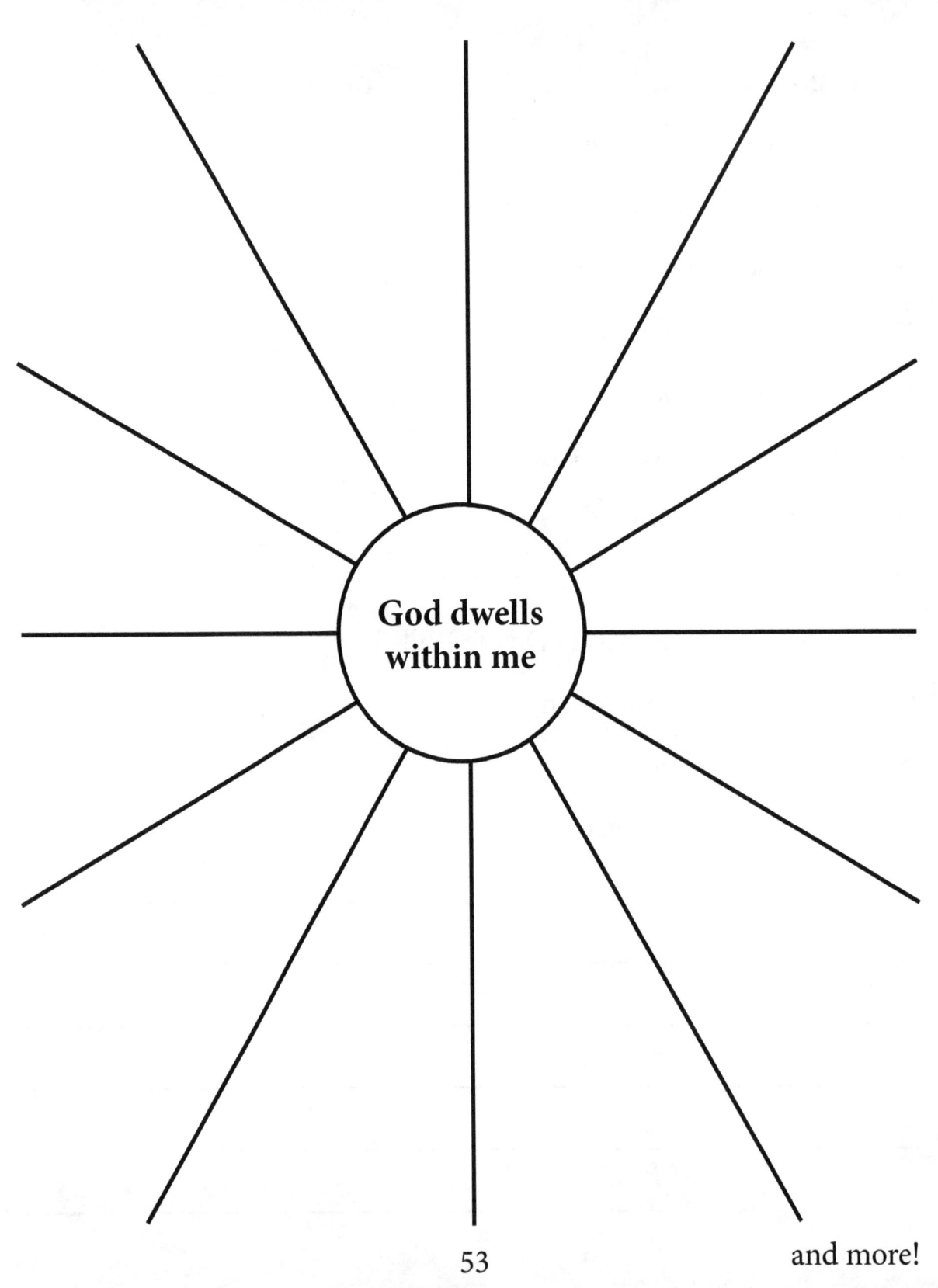

and more!

God dwells within me

- ♥ He left us with His Holy Spirit
- ♥ I feel the connection all the time
- ♥ I choose to connect to the power of the Holy Spirit within me
- ♥ My body is God's temple
- ♥ I dwell with God
- ♥ I feel His presence with goosebumps and inner guidance
- ♥ He is mine and I am His
- ♥ I have a God-shaped structure in my heart only God can fill
- ♥ He strengthens me and comforts me
- ♥ In my weakness He is strong
- ♥ God is always within me
- ♥ God and I are one

_____

_____

_____

_____

_____

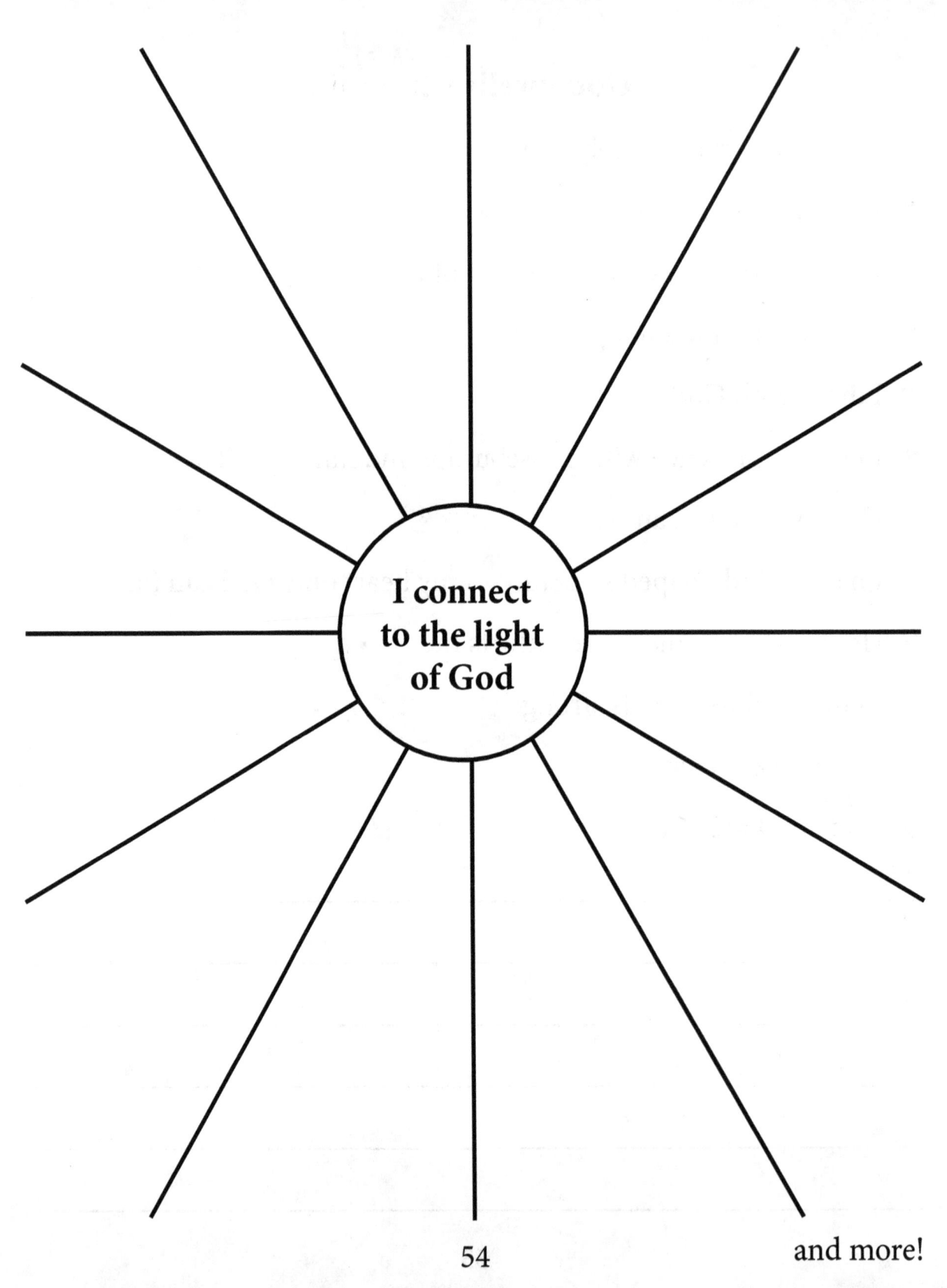

and more!

I connect to the light of God

- ♥ I pray daily
- ♥ I know myself and what I require
- ♥ I connect the moment my eyes open
- ♥ I seek Him first
- ♥ I meditate and listen to God
- ♥ I have a divine mission
- ♥ I am yoked to Christ
- ♥ I journal daily
- ♥ I rejoice in everything God has done for me
- ♥ I am a cheerful giver and receiver
- ♥ God's light shines through me
- ♥ I am filled with His light. I shine brightly

_____
_____
_____
_____
_____

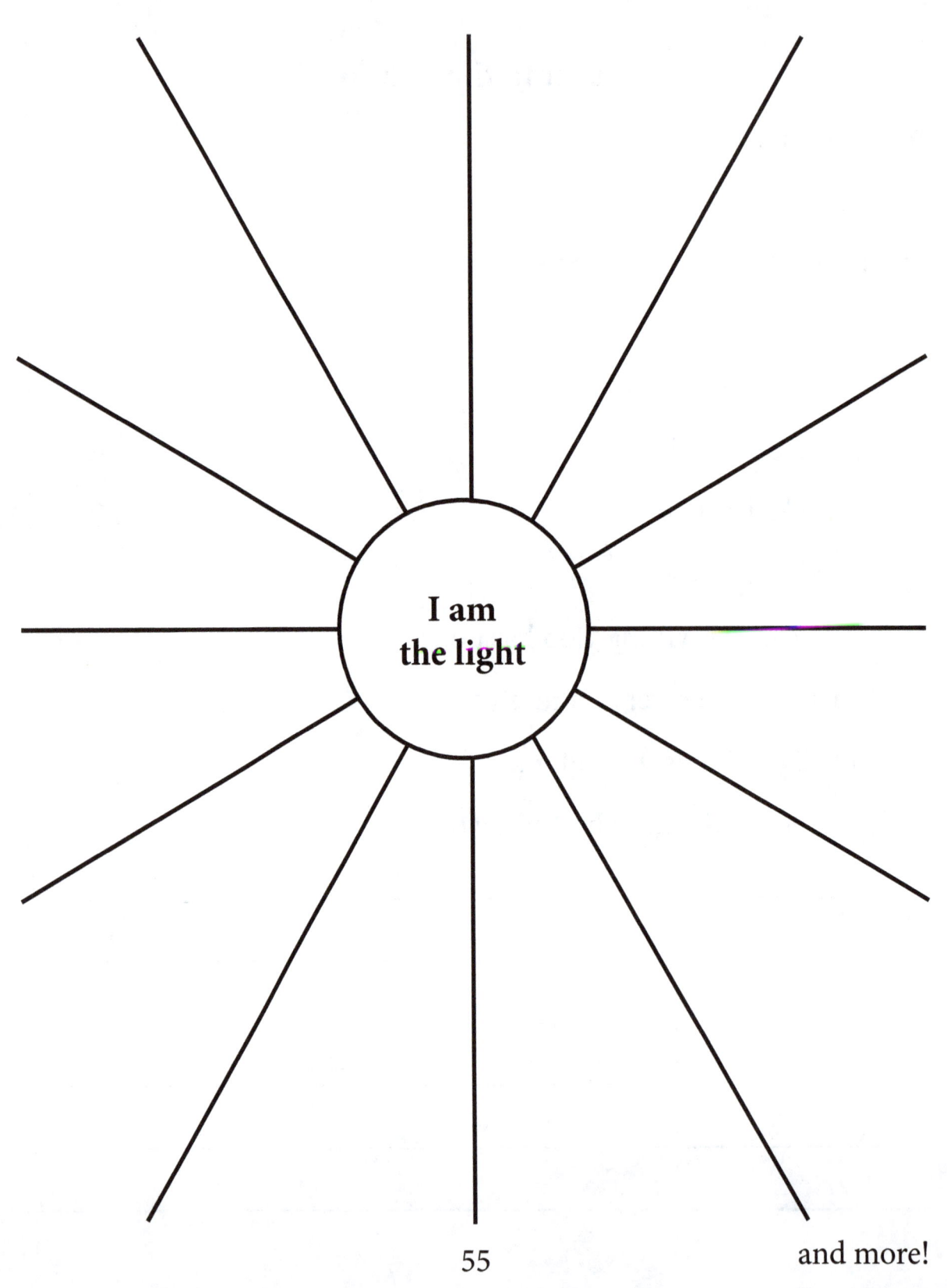

and more!

I am the light

- ♥ I choose positivity
- ♥ My mouth speaks what my heart is full of
- ♥ My cells are full of photon light energy, I am light energy
- ♥ My heart is full of compassion and my mouth is full of praise
- ♥ God's love and light shine through me out into the world
- ♥ I take it all to God in prayer and leave it there
- ♥ As Jesus is the light of the world I am His child and the fruit of His Tree of Life thus I am also the light
- ♥ God said let there be light and there is light in every atom
- ♥ I am particle, wave, and energy
- ♥ I am more than my physical body
- ♥ I feel God's light everywhere
- ♥ I am connected to God, I am yoked to Him

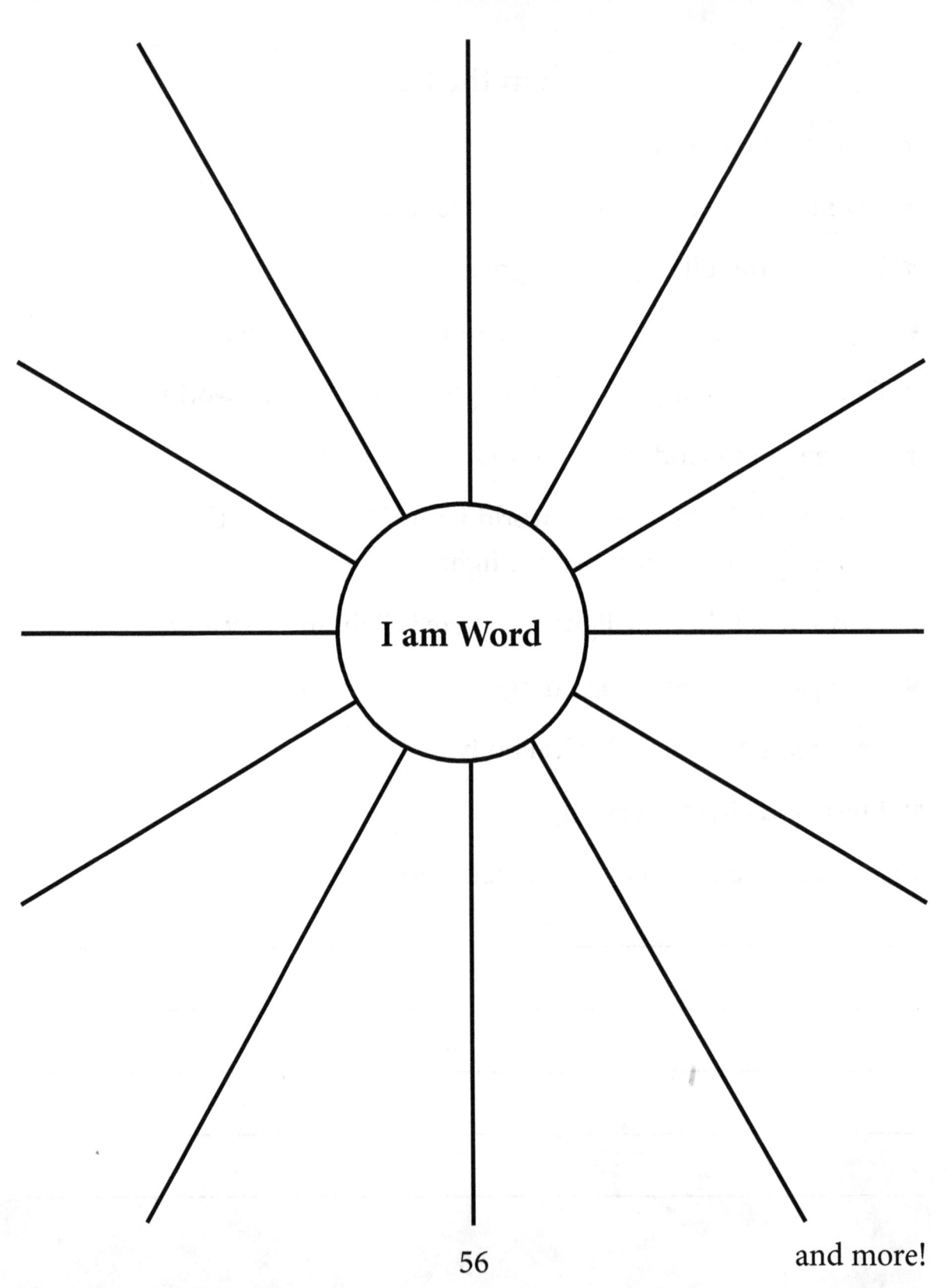

I am Word

- ♥ The words coming from my mouth are seeds sown that will be reaped
- ♥ Creation power is in the word
- ♥ Every word that leaves our mouth comes back answered
- ♥ We are God's favorite creation
- ♥ Humans are the only creatures that speak words
- ♥ God spoke everything into existence
- ♥ Jesus healed with His words
- ♥ We are made in His image and likeness
- ♥ Our words hold vibration power
- ♥ Words create. My words call things into my life
- ♥ The more beautiful my words the more beautiful and wonderful is my life
- ♥ I am Word, I am Word, I am Word, so be it

_____
_____
_____
_____

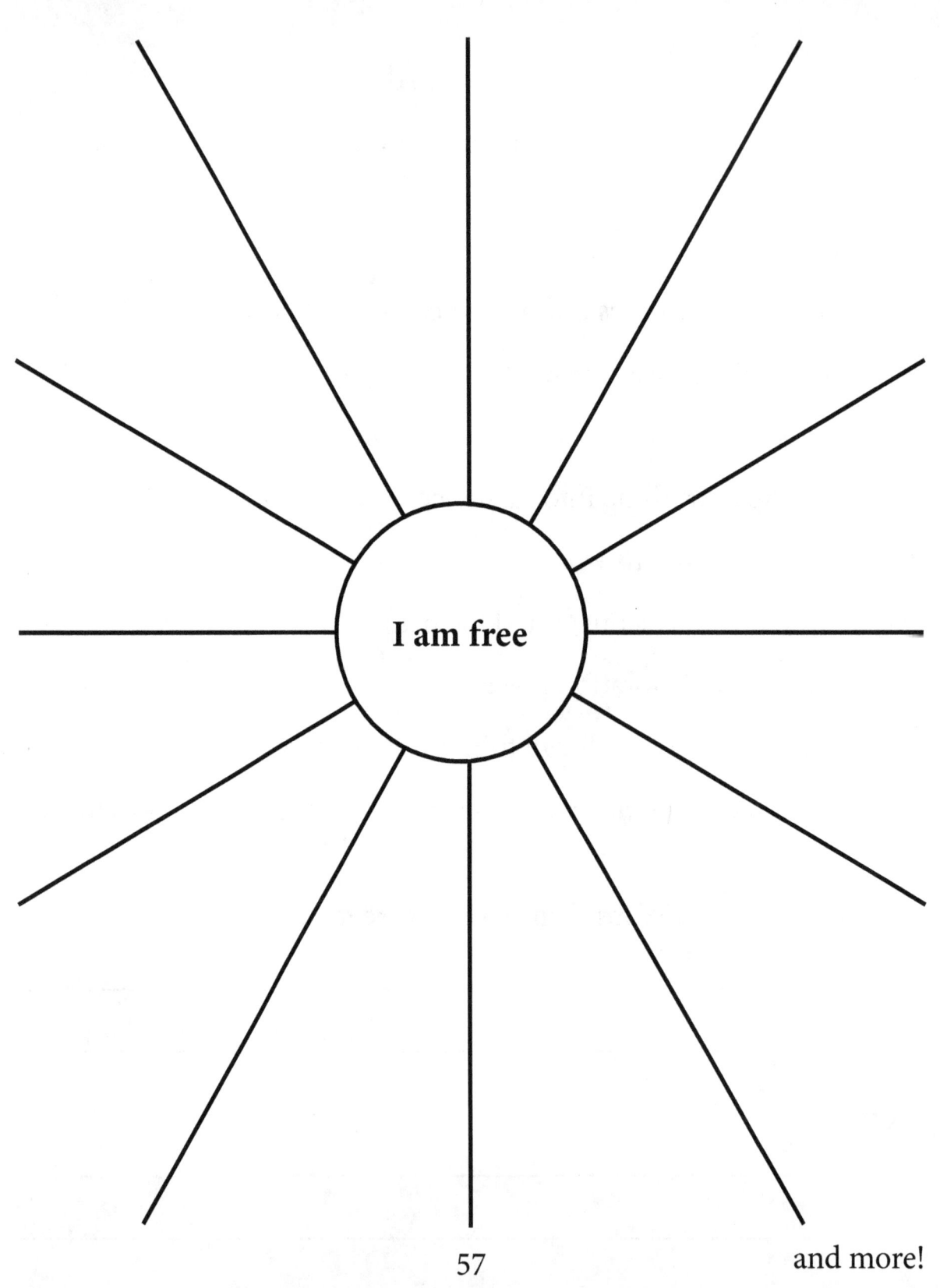

and more!

I am free

- ♥ I am free indeed
- ♥ My heart is wide open
- ♥ I expect miracles in every moment
- ♥ My life is light and easy
- ♥ I am in charge of my thoughts and words
- ♥ I attract goodness all around me
- ♥ I am open for abundance in every area of my life
- ♥ I am free to rejoice
- ♥ Freedom feels wonderful
- ♥ My only yoke is to Christ
- ♥ I am in this world yet of God's world
- ♥ I accept the supernatural wonders of God

_____
_____
_____
_____
_____

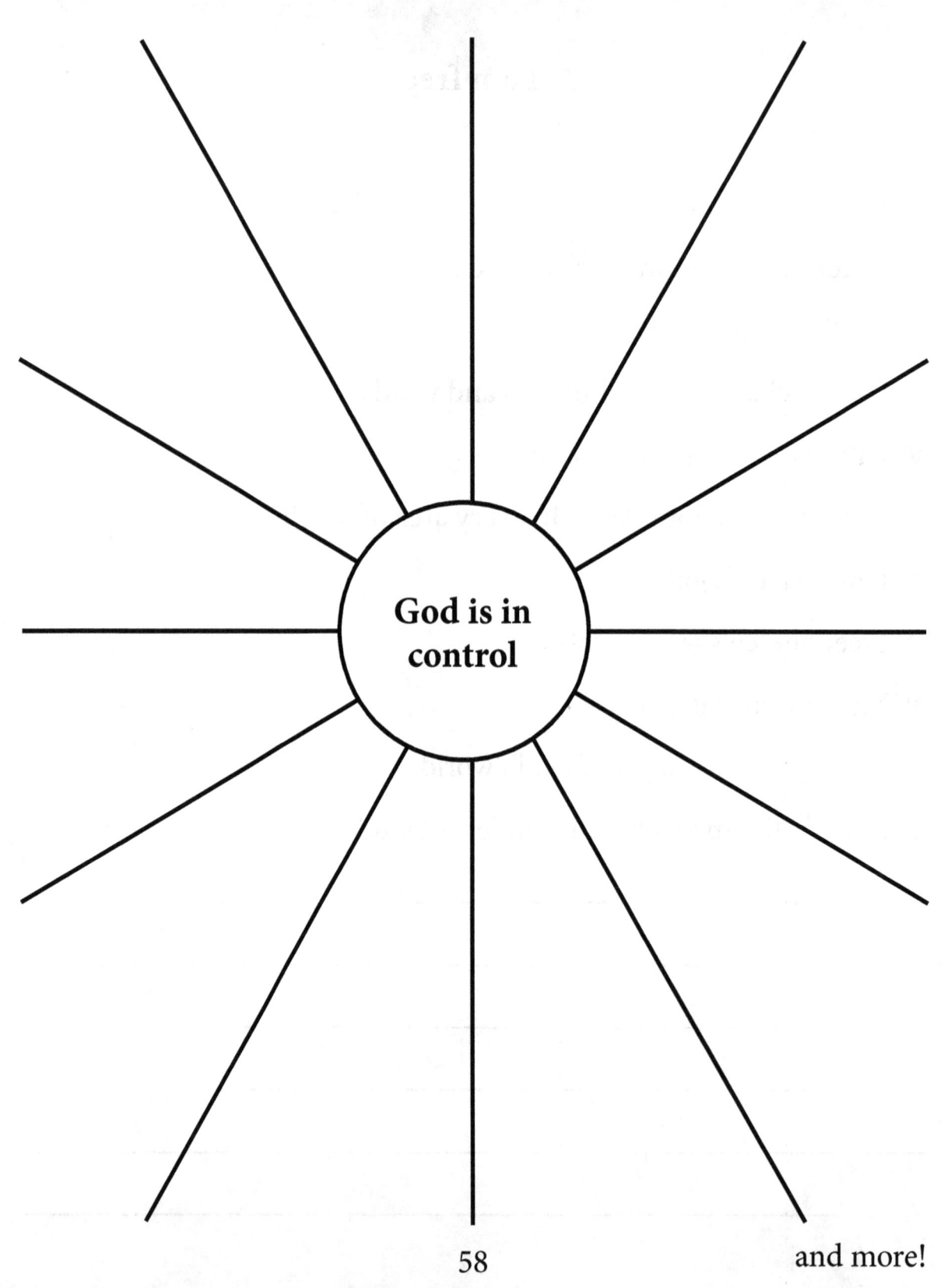

God is in control

- ♥ The Bible tells me to lean unto His heavenly understanding
- ♥ I trust in God's power and His desire for me to prosper
- ♥ He planned everything from the beginning to the end
- ♥ He has a perfect track record
- ♥ He is the miracle maker
- ♥ God is the Alpha and the Omega, He is the beginning and the end.
- ♥ God created man
- ♥ God created everything
- ♥ Whether I am here or beyond the sun still shines and the seasons progress
- ♥ God knows every feather on a sparrow and every hair on my head
- ♥ His mercy and grace cover me like a garment of light
- ♥ I am one with my Father who created me

_____

_____

_____

_____

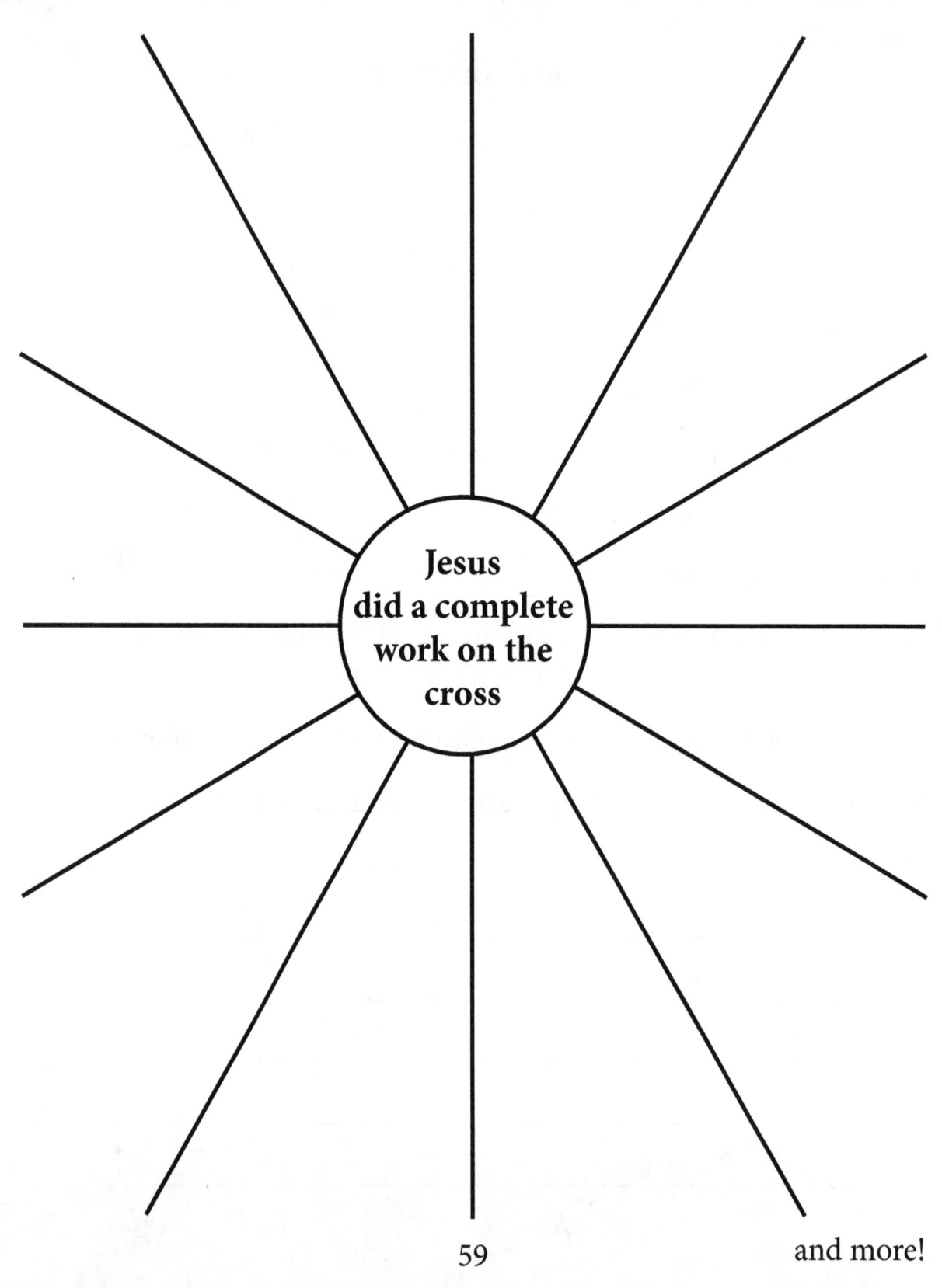

and more!

Jesus did a complete work on the cross

- ♥ It is finished
- ♥ Paid in full
- ♥ I am now saved by grace
- ♥ I am now perfect in His eyes
- ♥ God loves me so much
- ♥ He wishes for me to have a happy and joyful life
- ♥ Grace and mercy abound
- ♥ Rejoice, again I say rejoice
- ♥ He is coming to celebrate with us at His wedding feast
- ♥ I am complete in Him
- ♥ He lives in the Tree of Life and desires me to live there with Him
- ♥ I am free

_____

_____

_____

_____

_____

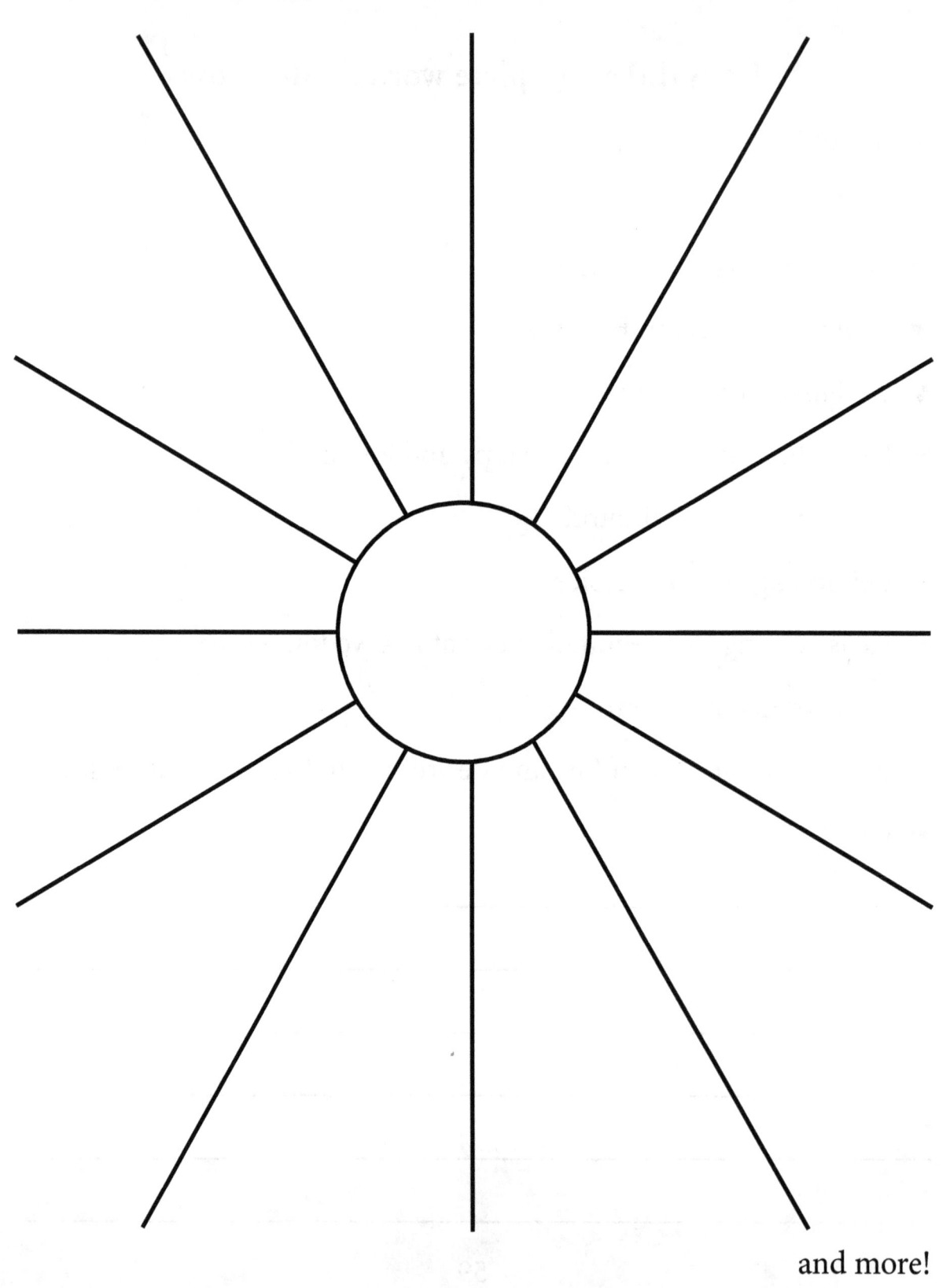

and more!

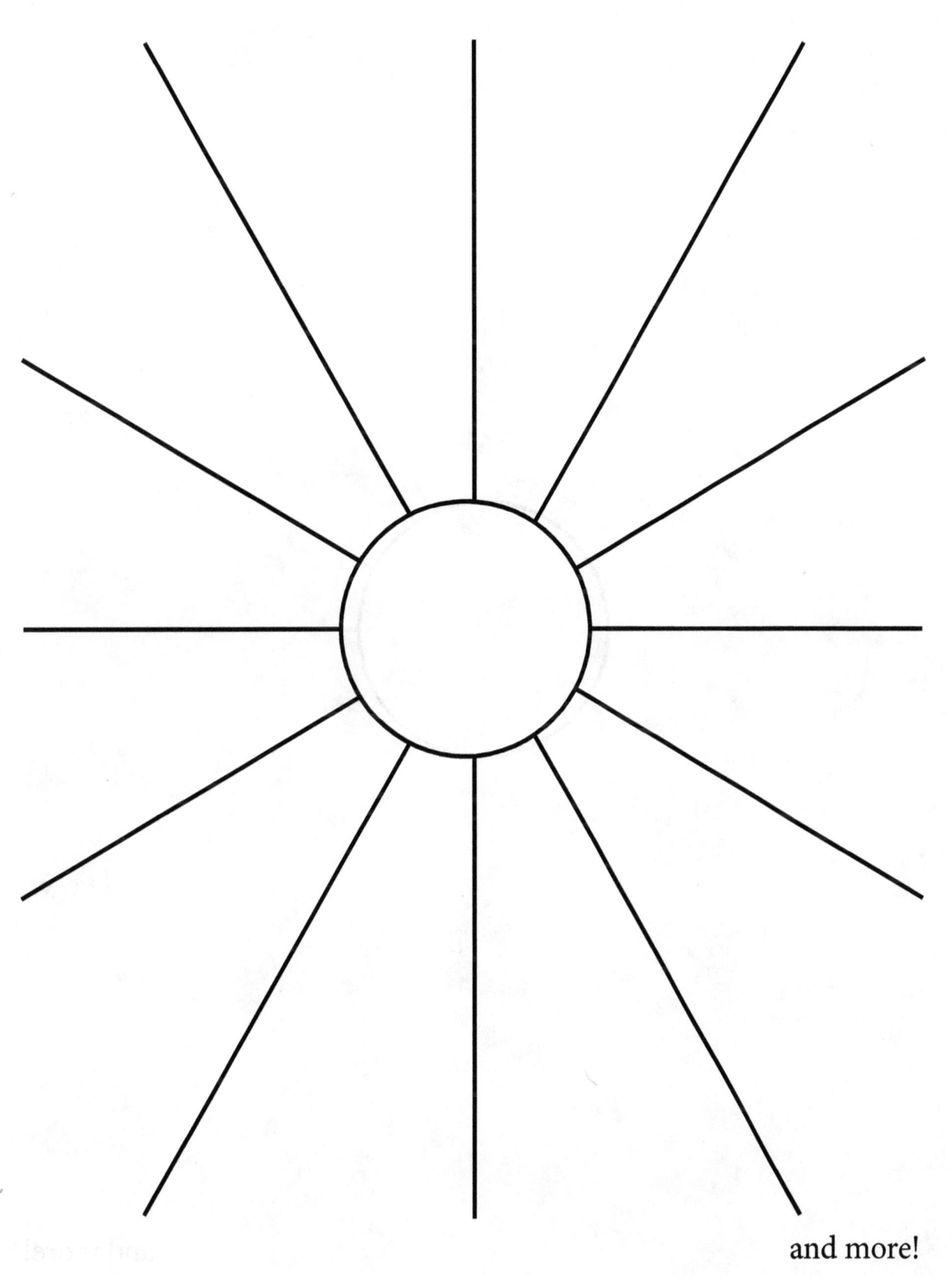

and more!

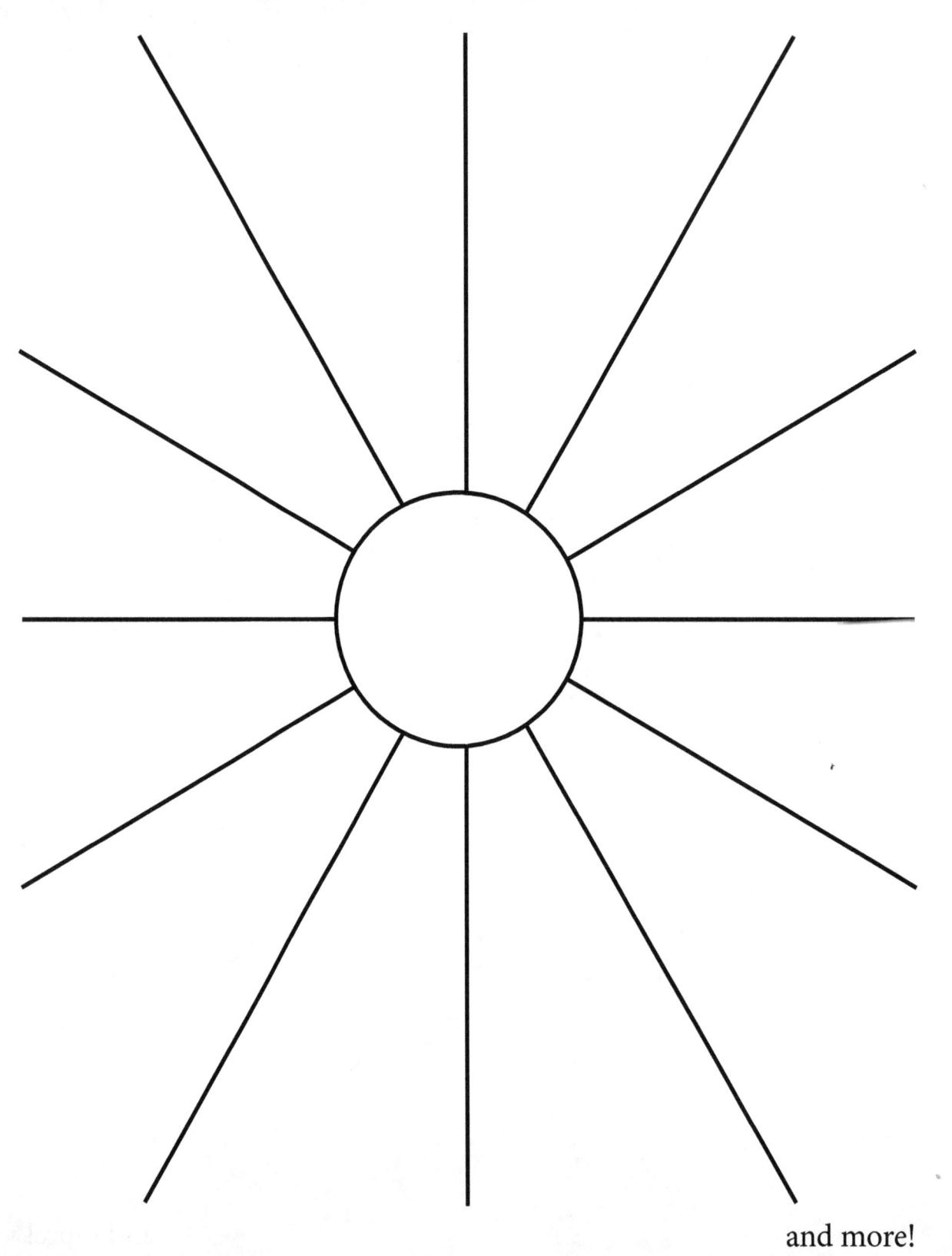

and more!

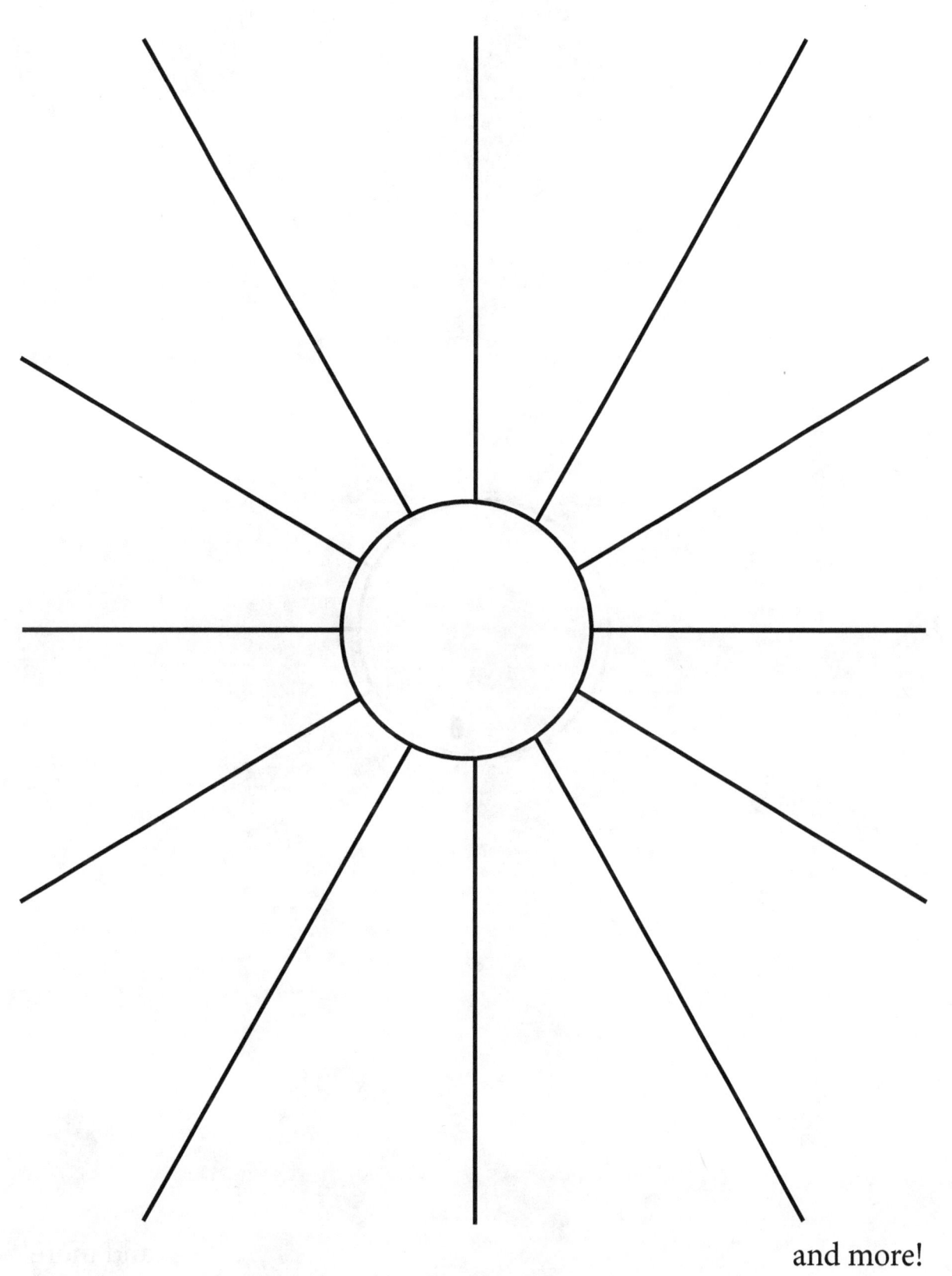

and more!

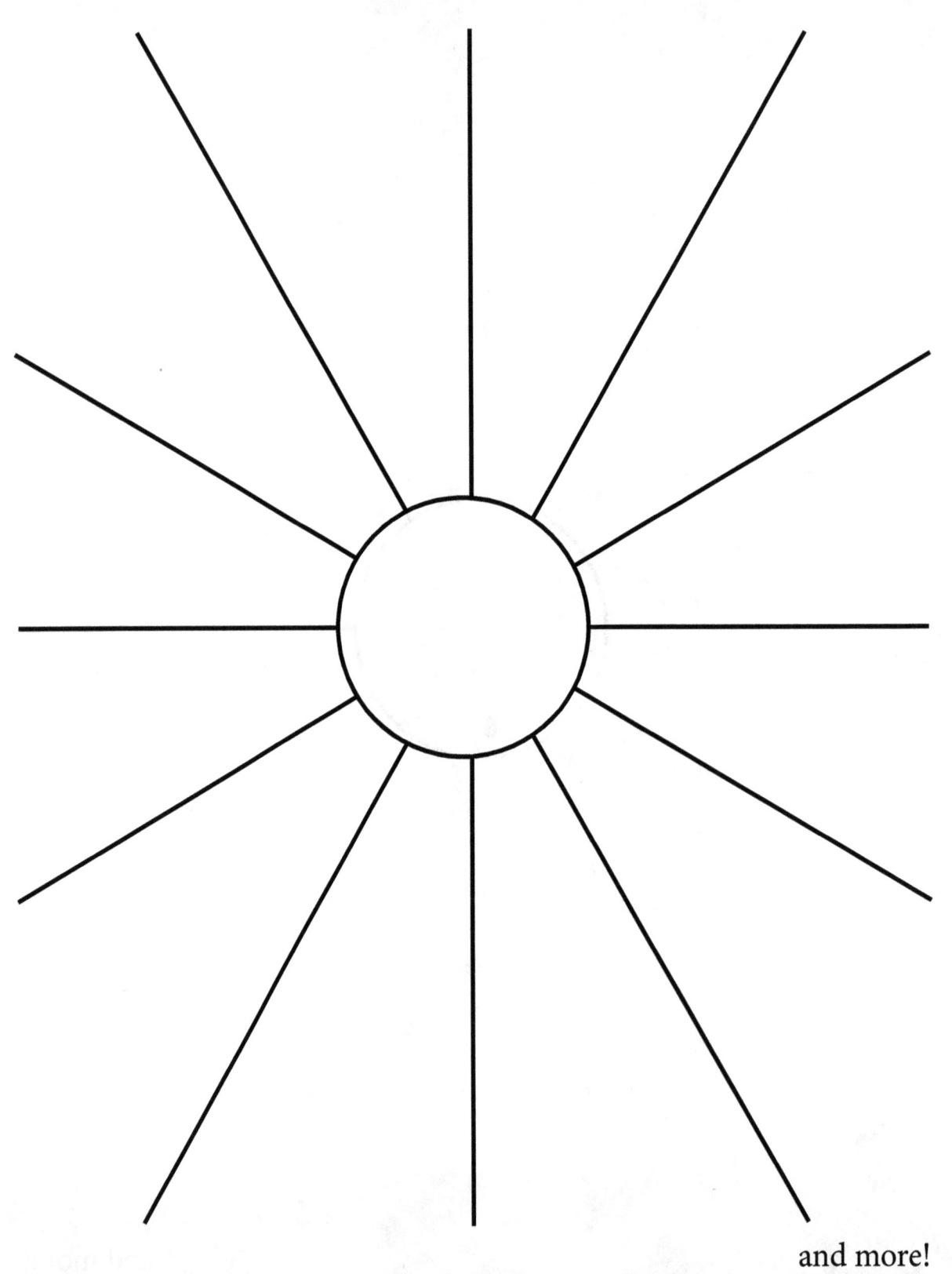

and more!

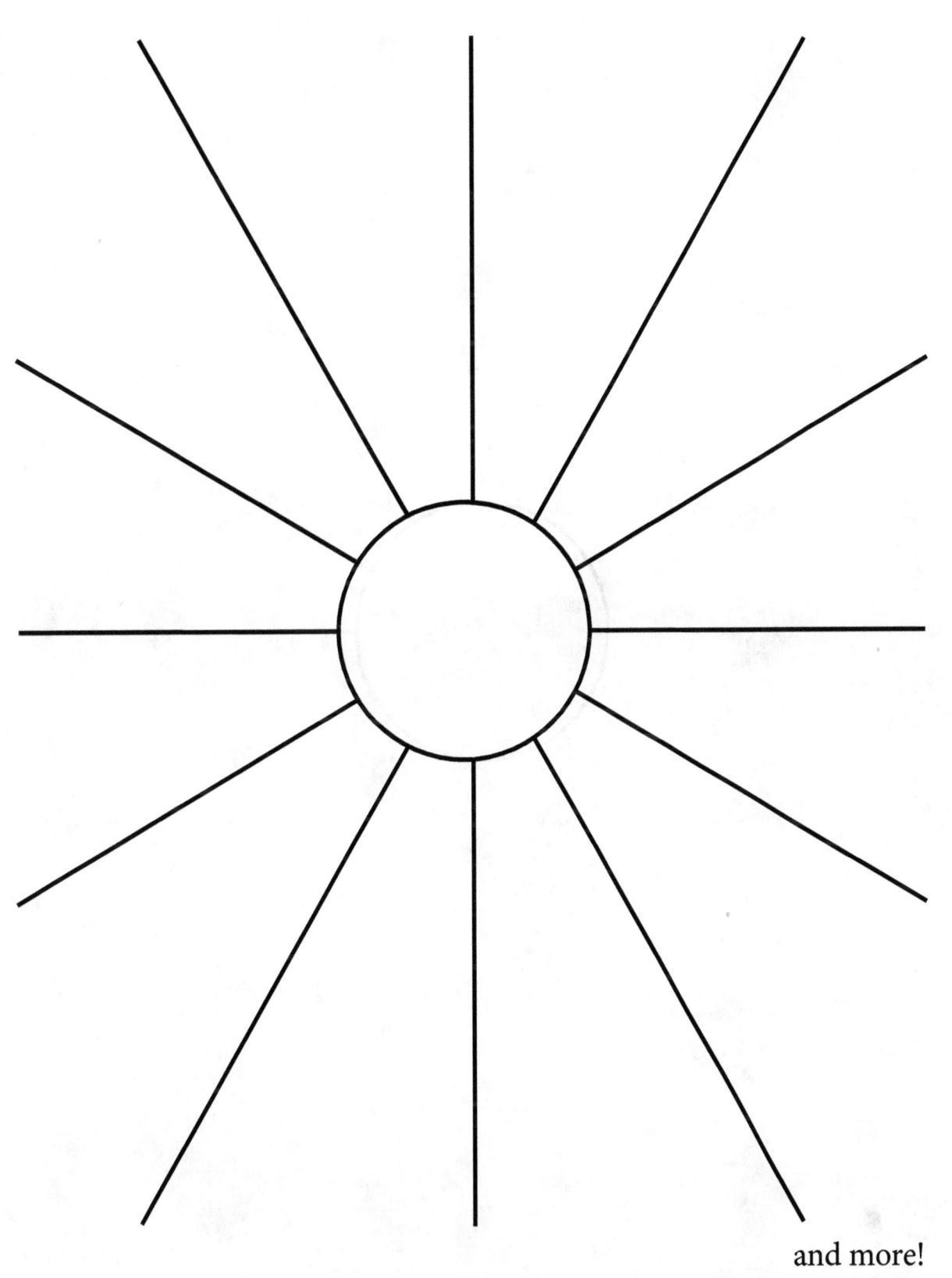

and more!

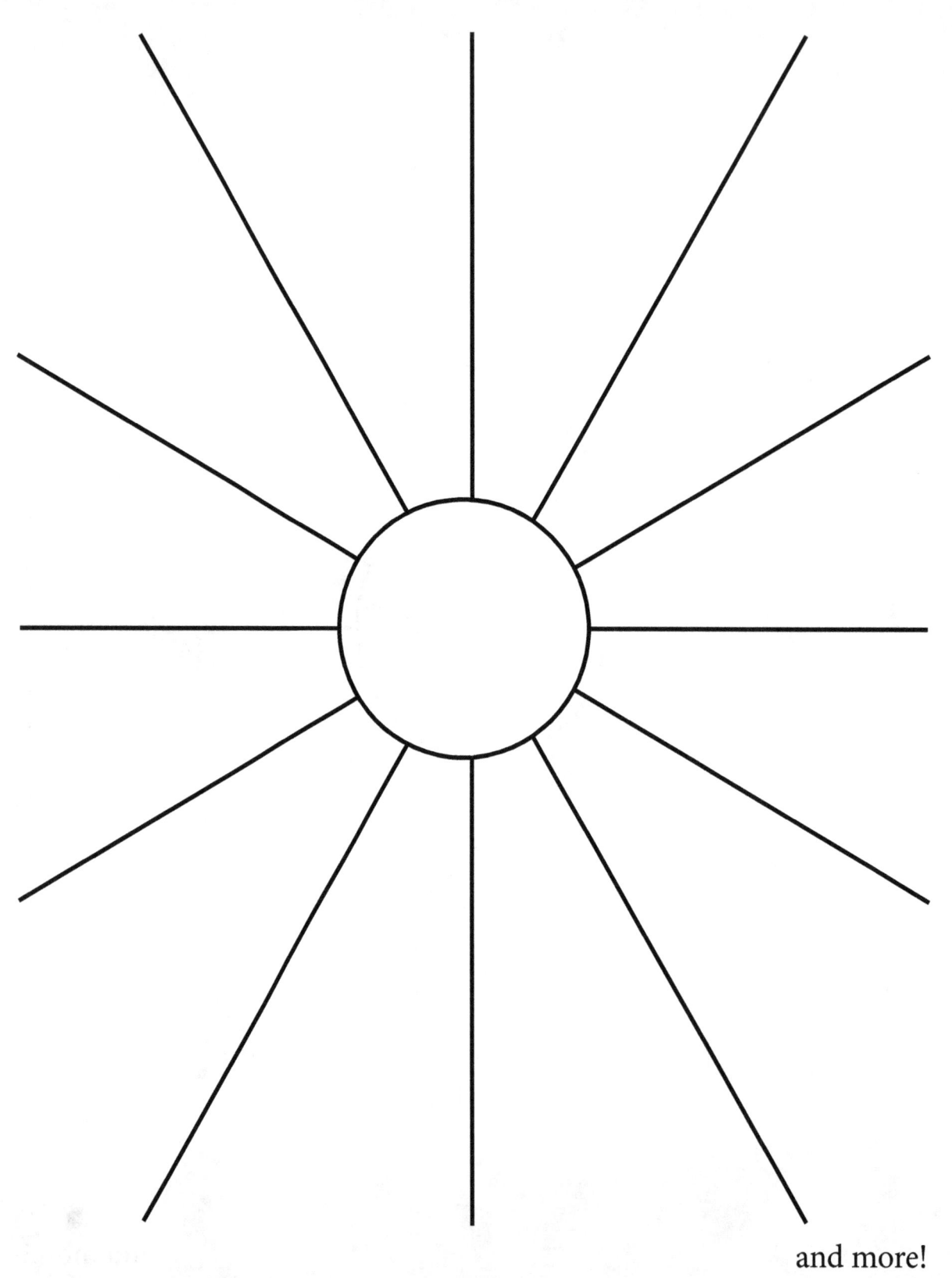

and more!

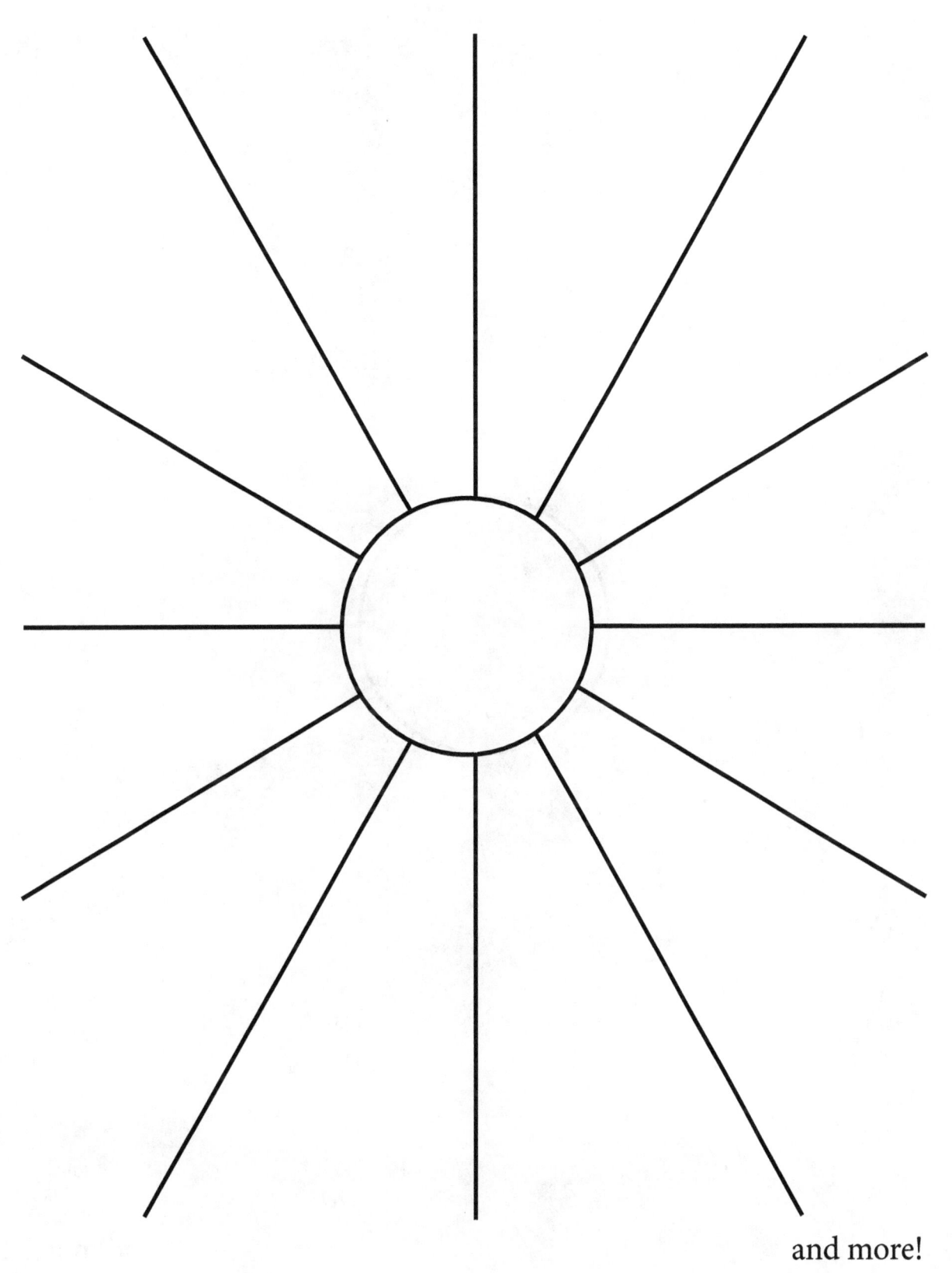

and more!

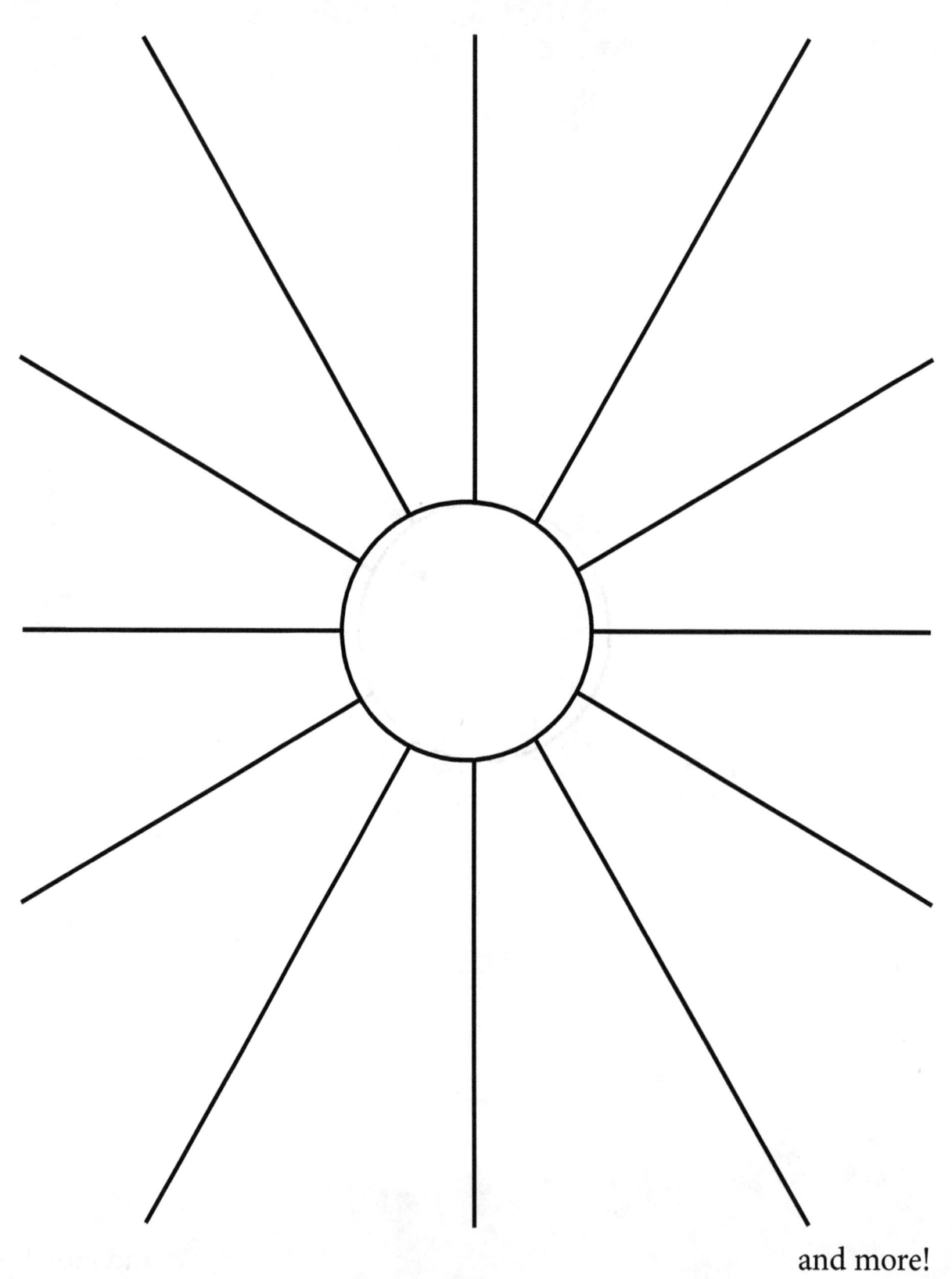

and more!

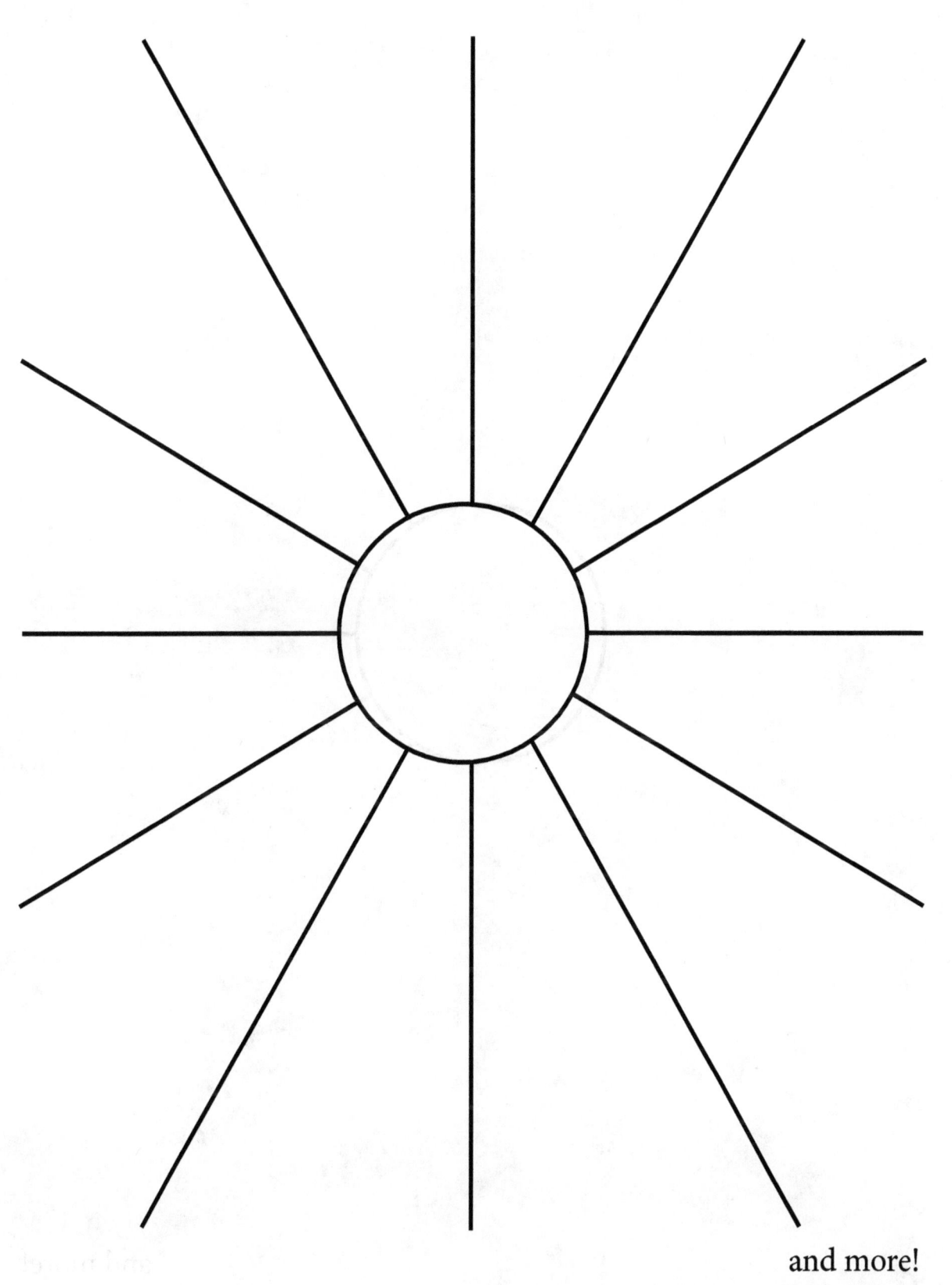

and more!

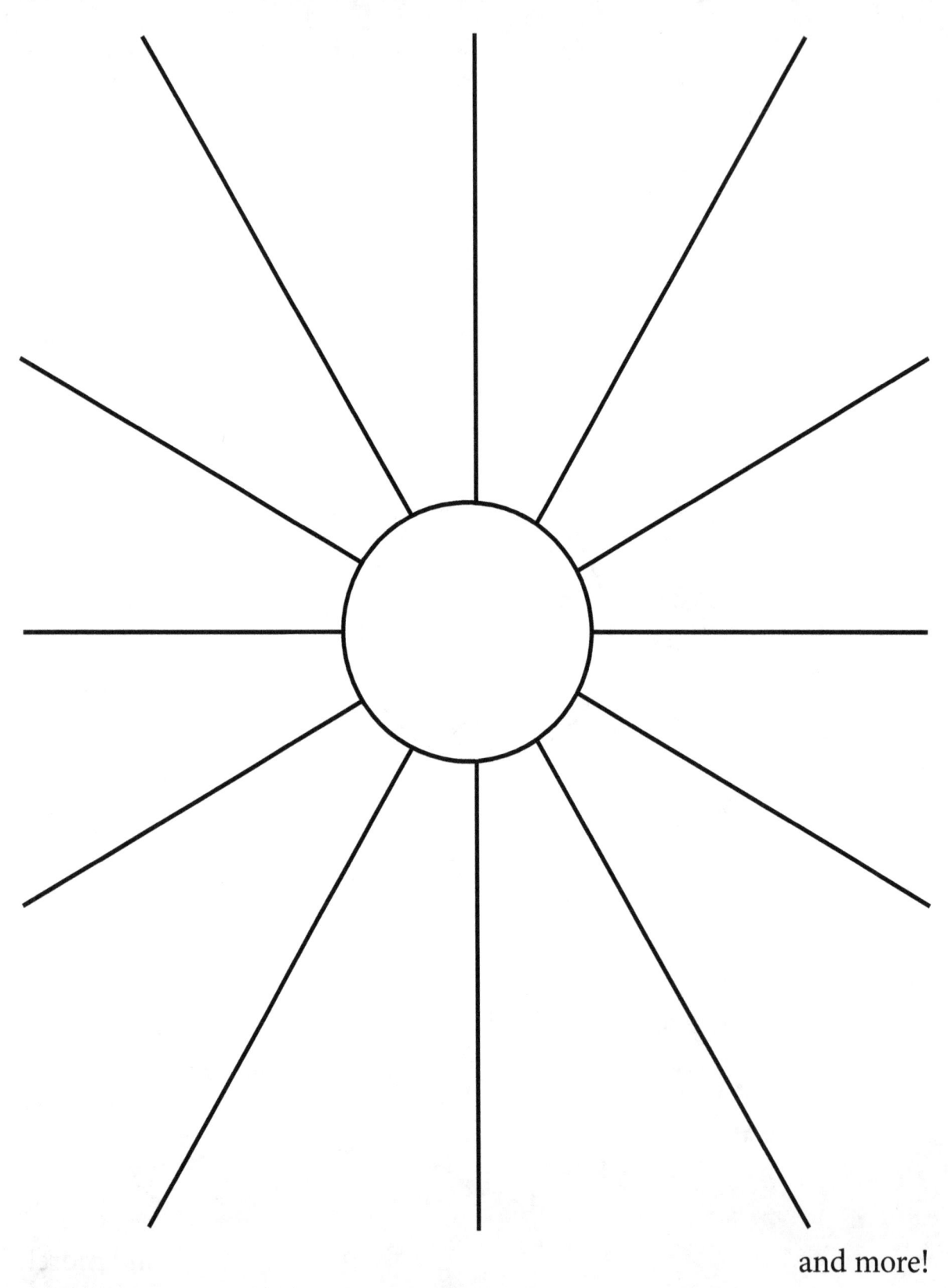

and more!

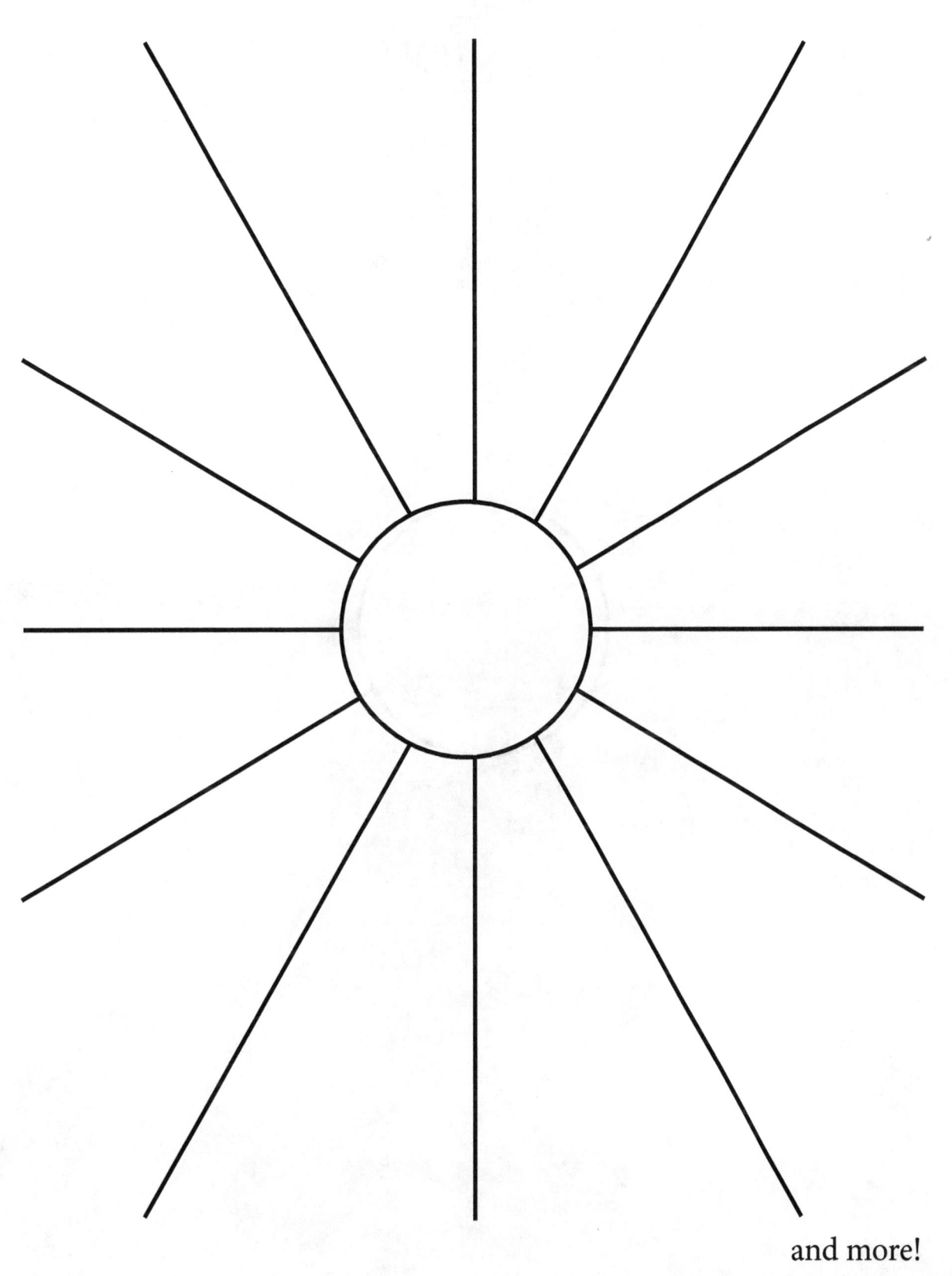

and more!

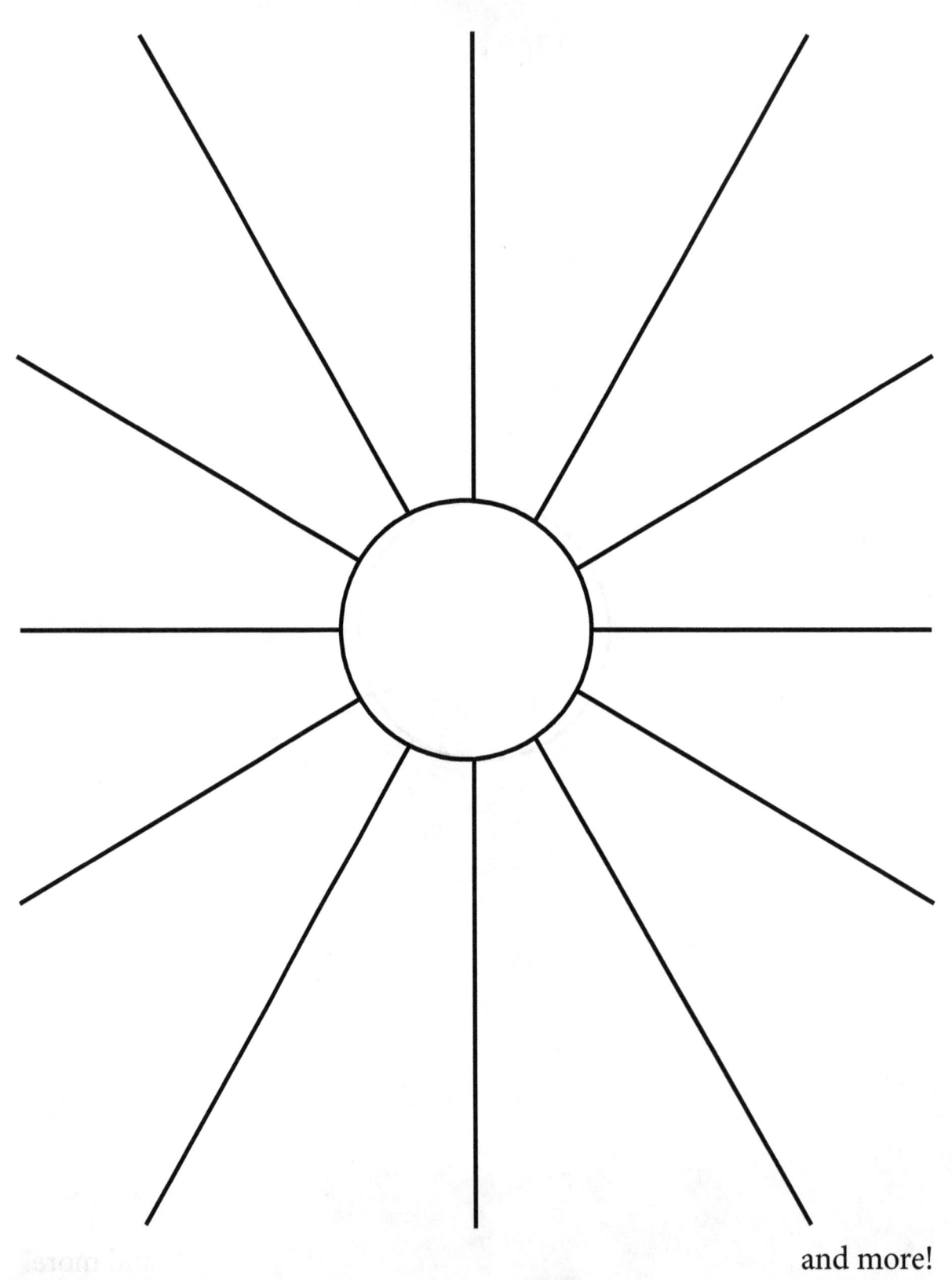

and more!

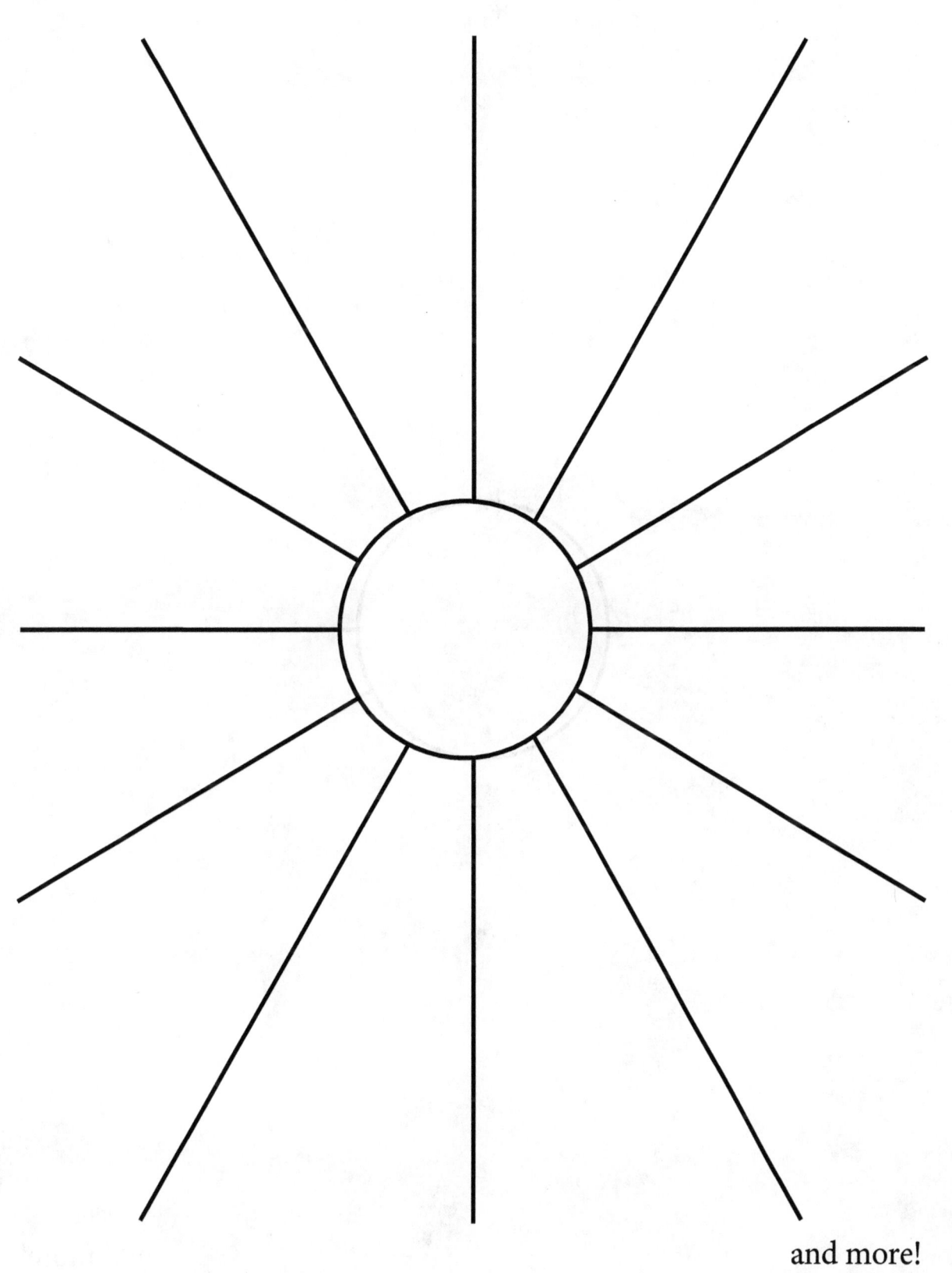

and more!

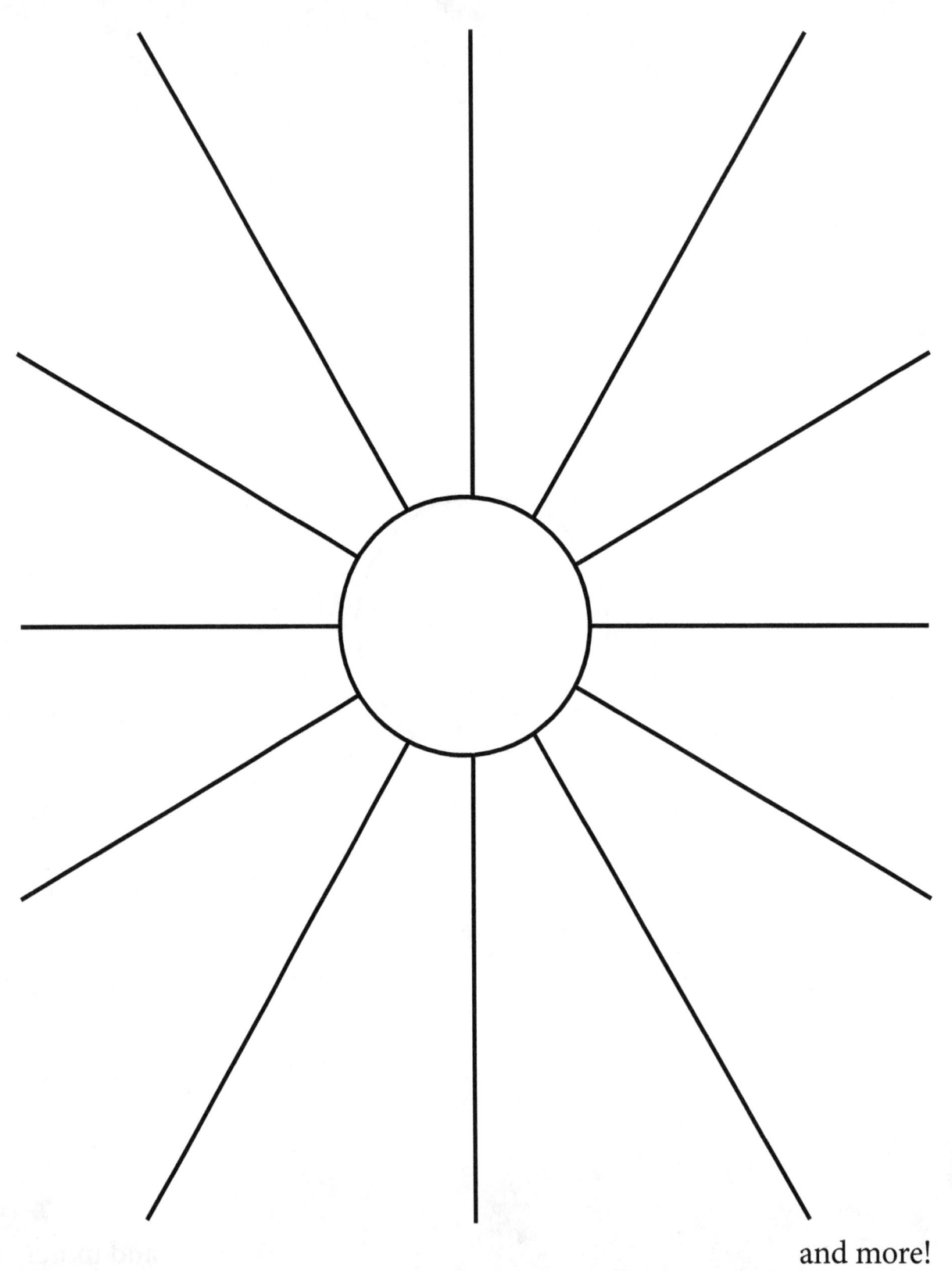

and more!

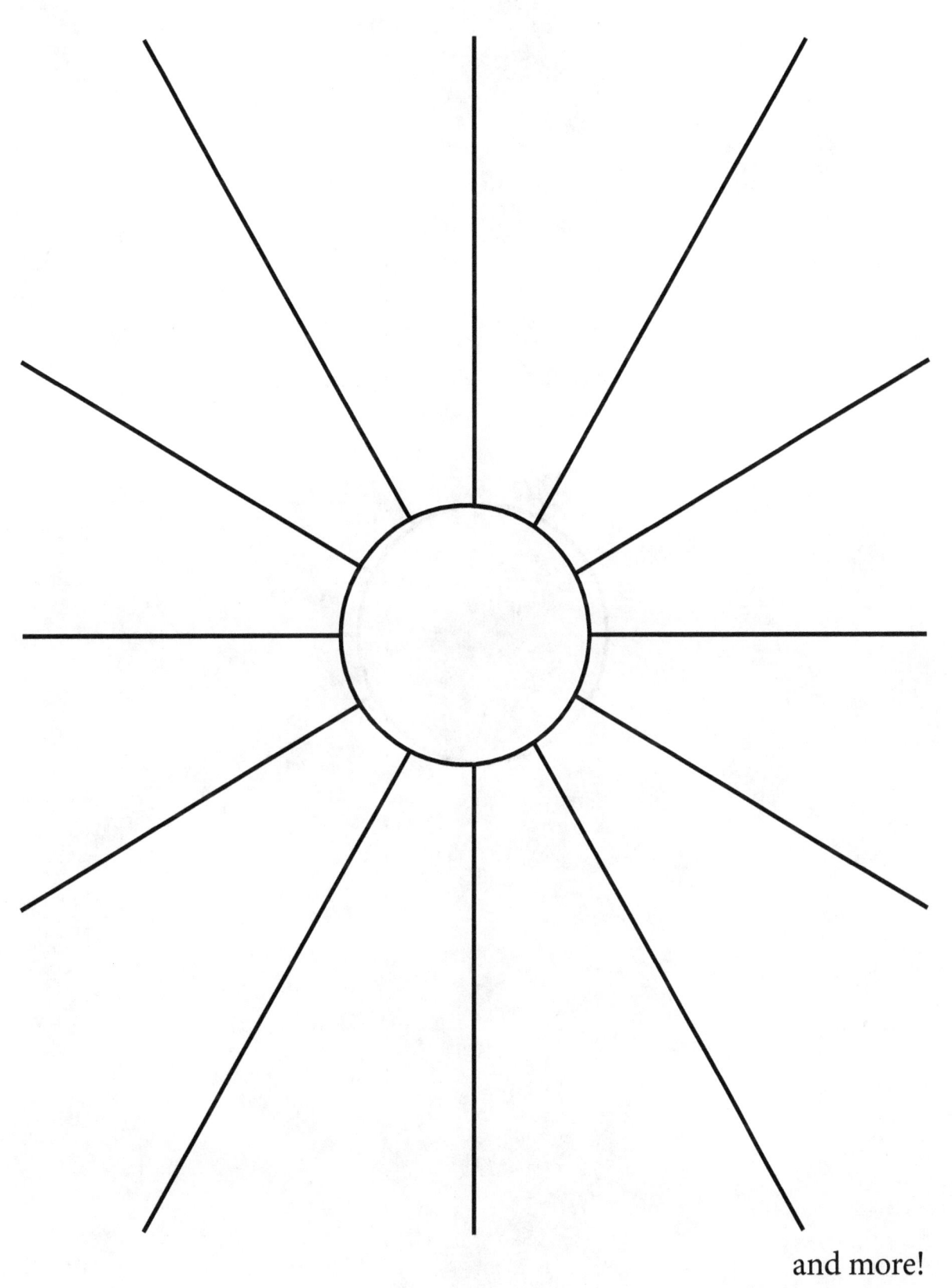

and more!

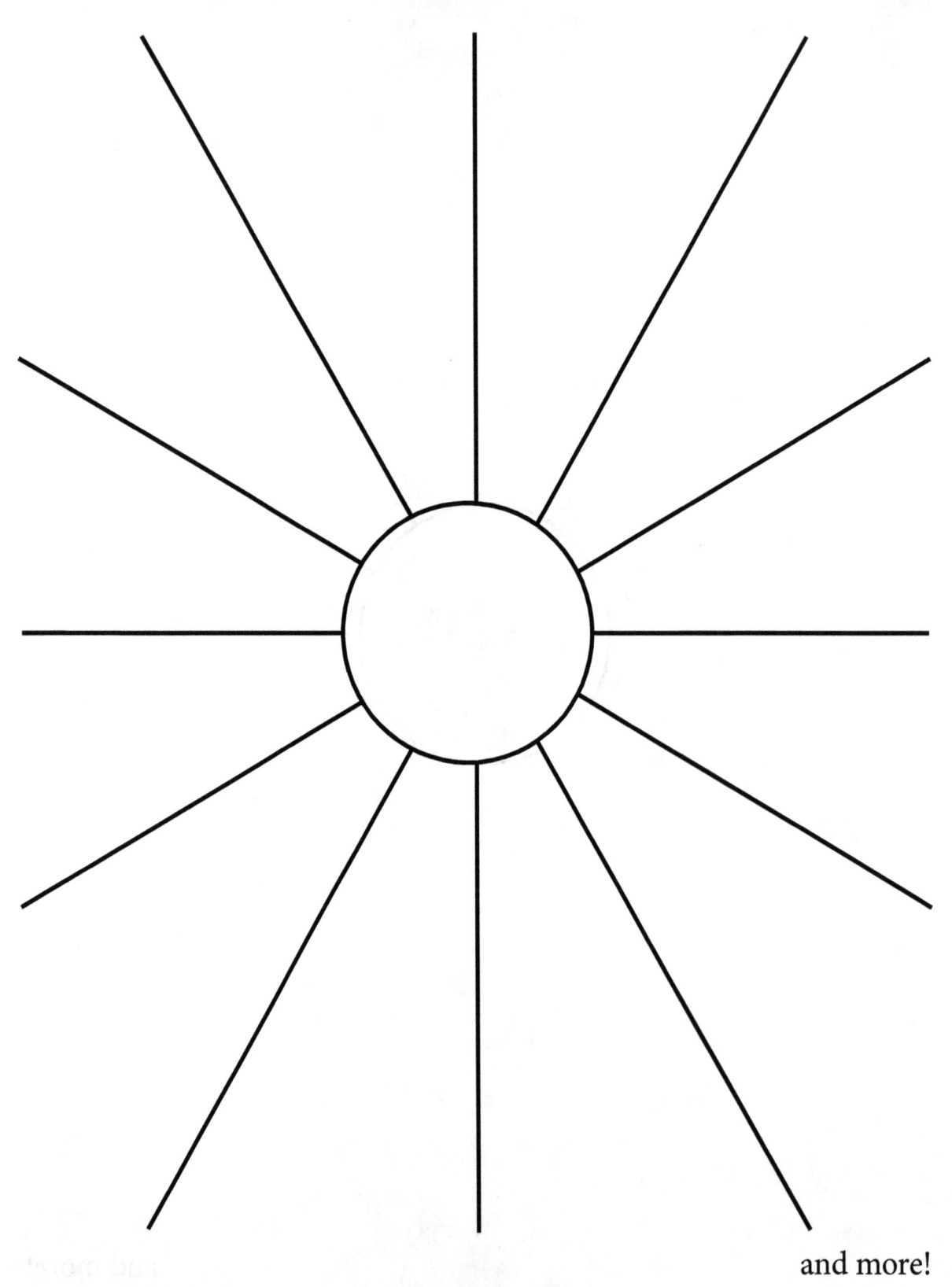

and more!

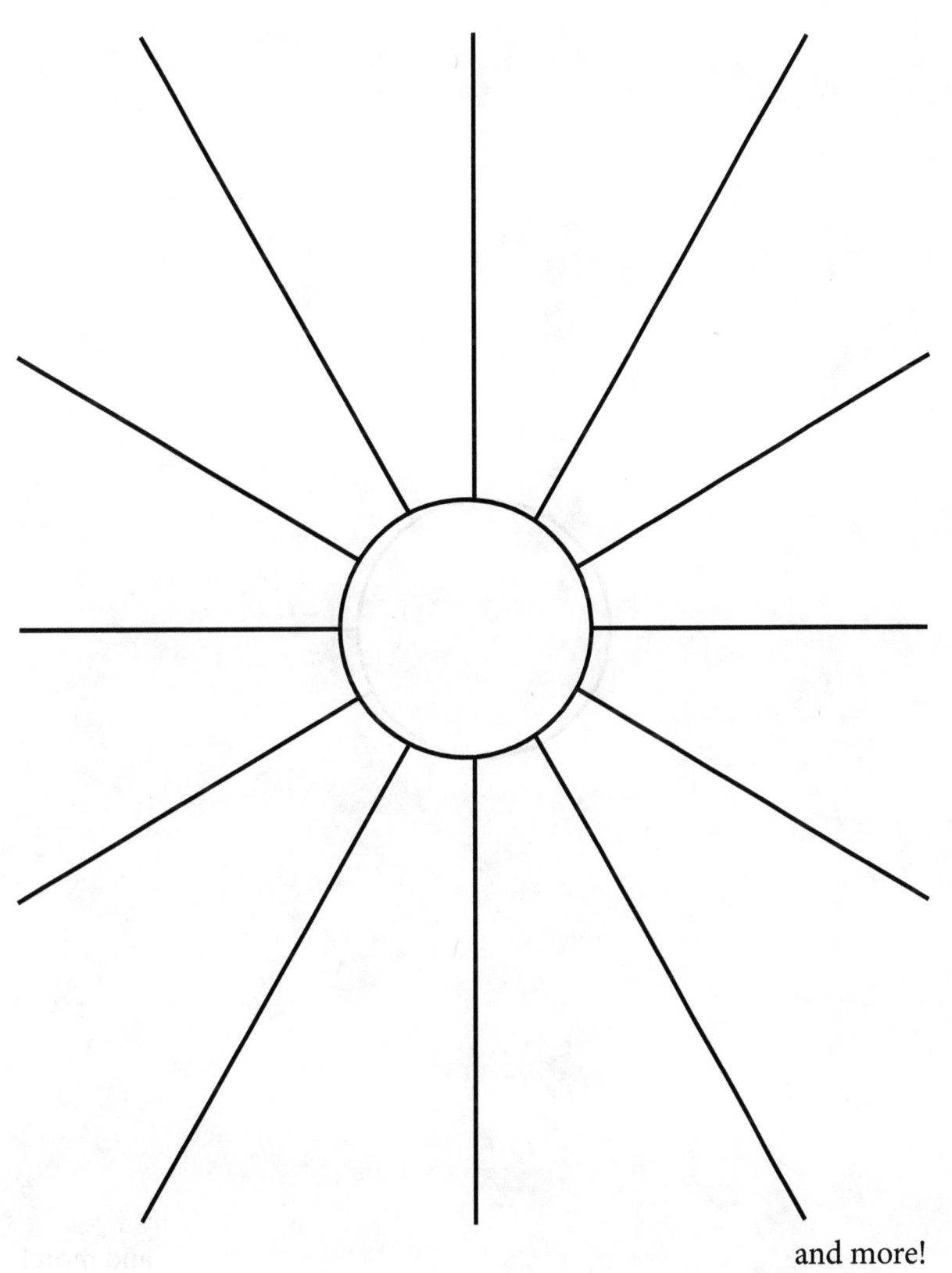

and more!

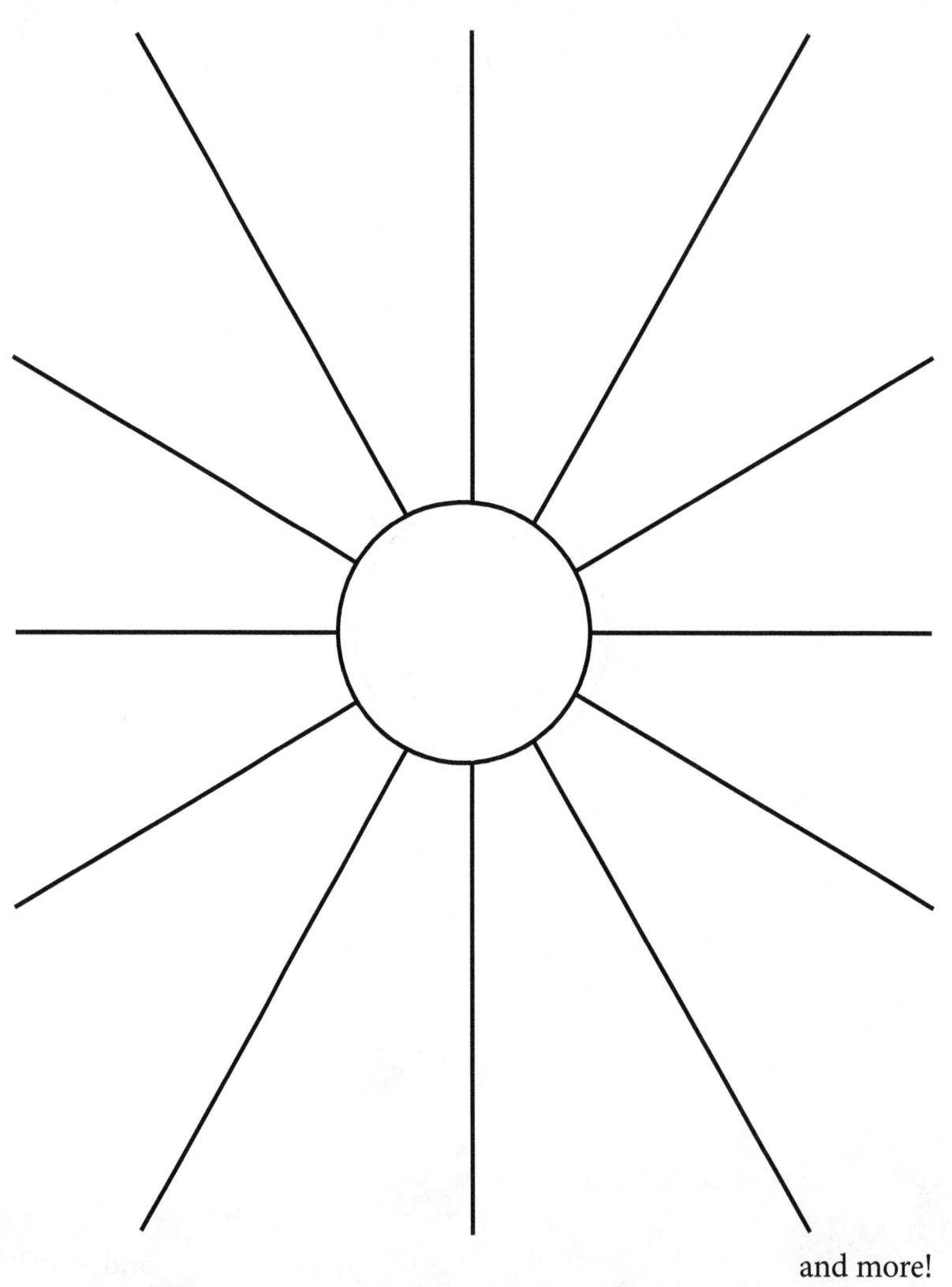
and more!

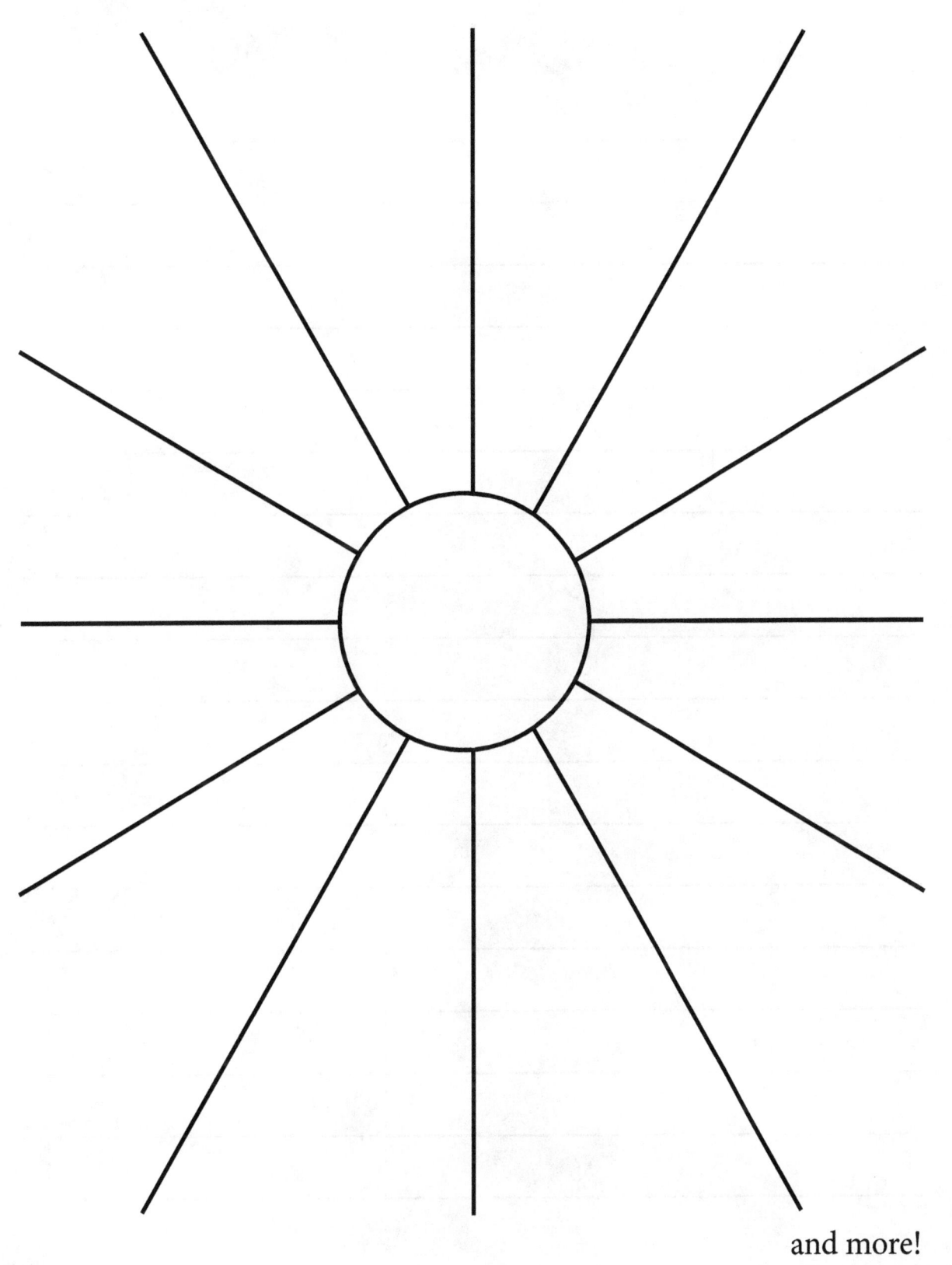

and more!

Notes

Notes

Notes

Notes

Notes

Notes

Notes

Notes

Notes

Notes

AVAILABLE FROM RECEIVE JOY

ASK AND YOU SHALL RECEIVE

The Power of Positive Words
+ the Law of Attraction
+ God
= Your Light and Easy Life!

This is "the secret beyond the secret"! This book will help encourage you to create and define a direction and plan for your life. I wish to share my Nine Step Method to empower everyone to feel the freedom of a light and easy life. Open your heart and your mind and journey with me to a new and more powerful, focused and loved, aware and connected You.

$15 (Amazon $20)
ISBN: 978-0-9988484-8-8

ASK AND YOU SHALL RECEIVE MEDITATION

Enjoy this 20-minute *Ask And You Shall Receive Meditation* in all positive words—listen to the truth about yourself and receive inspiration.

$5
UPC: 098867225629

DAILY ASKING JOURNAL
Live by Design!

To make your life light and easy, let us put the Nine Step Method into daily action by using the *Daily Asking Journal*. This Journal will help connect you with the Power of the Universe and enable you to collect and compile all your asking intentions in one place. This personal journal for your focused thoughts and positive words supports you to raise your awareness, while having an organized platform to consciously create and record your positive, happy, light, and easy life. Script your life, keep on asking God, and be a new wineskin.

$10 (Amazon $12)
ISBN: 978-0-9988484-0-2

INSPIRATION NOTEBOOK

Live inspired!

The *Inspiration Notebook* is designed as a platform to create and record your inspirations and highlights, ideas and insights, goals and plans. Daily writing enables you to experience a purposeful life with clarity. Your ongoing plans of action and written insights guide you toward your goals and direct all focus on your target. Let this personal journal hold your ideas and goals.

The *Inspiration Notebook* is a tool to help you measure your continual growth and accomplishments. Pick up a pen, and script your life in your own hand.

$10 (Amazon $12)
ISBN: 978-0-9988484-2-6

CONNECT TO THE LIGHT

We charge our cellphone, plug in the toaster and the hairdryer, let us also plug our life in first. Step one in the process of truly deciding to make changes in our life and begin living by design starts with the understanding that we are connected to the greatest Power Source there is—God. Let us consciously connect first and harness this power. Once we are connected, our life starts to flow.

Connect To The Light provides ways to maintain our connection to the light energy and to live by conscious design. Let us be heavenly-minded, yet of earthly use.

$20 (Amazon $20)
ISBN: 978-0-9988484-1-9

RECEIVE INSPIRATION

Receive Inspiration contains a mix of inspirations to open the mind to receive happiness, love, prosperity, well-being, growth, focus, and allowing. Receive Joy created this encouraging CD using only positive words that we may consciously choose to remember our greatness. Let us cheer ourselves on! Be inspired!

CD, $10
UPC: 098867227227

RECEIVE BEAUTIFUL WORDS

Every word is a creation. We can choose to create love, joy, gratitude, hope, compassion, mercy, praise and much more positivity with our words. Let us be conscious of which word we send out to achieve what we desire. Play *Receive Beautiful Words* to imprint ourselves and our environment with positive blessings. Listen and Receive Joy!

CD, $10
UPC: 098867227128

All products are available directly from Receive Joy.

To learn more visit **www.receivejoy.com**

Subscribe to our newsletter to continue your receiving of positive awareness. Please share your email address with us: **ask@receivejoy.com**

Call or text to US cell phone number
(239) 450-1240

Like and follow Receive Joy on Facebook:
www.facebook.com/ReceiveJoy

Follow Receive Joy on Instagram:
www.instagram.com/receivejoy

We are happy to hear from you and receive your positive feedback, inspiration, and miracle stories!

With Love and Gratitude,

www.ingramcontent.com/pod-product-compliance
Lightning Source LLC
Chambersburg PA
CBHW080403170426
43193CB00016B/2789